Did Pirates Rip Her Arms Off?

Did Pirates Rip Her Arms Off?

an Anthology

edited by

Robert Kane
Stephanie Halpern
&
Spencer Seward

Red Hen Press | *Pasadena, CA*

Book layout by Spencer Seward
Additional copy editing by William Goldstein and Chris Konish
ISBN: 978-1-59709-495-5

The Audrey and Sydney Irmas Foundation, Dwight Stuart Youth Fund, Kinder Morgan Foundation, Sony Pictures Entertainment, Ralphs, and Target partially support Red Hen Press's Writing in the Schools program.

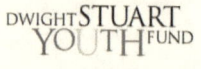

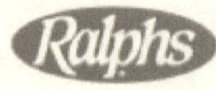

First Edition
Published by Red Hen Press
www.redhen.org

Acknowledgments

"Invention" by Frances Payne Adler. Published in *The Making of a Matriot* © Red Hen Press, 2003. Reprinted by permission of the author.

"Eureka Vacuum" by Erinn Batykefer. Published in *Allegheny, Monongahela* © Red Hen Press, 2009. Reprinted by permission of the author.

"Maid of Honor" by Elizabeth Bradfield. Published in *Interpretive Work* © Red Hen Press/Arktoi Books, 2008. Reprinted by permission of the author.

"Being Lon Chaney, Jr." by Gaylord Brewer. Published in *Barbaric Mercies* © Red Hen Press, 2003. Reprinted by permission of the author.

"The Proper Wolf" by Ron Carlson. Published in *Hunger Mountain* © Vermont College of Fine Arts, 2008. Reprinted by permission of the author.

"Cleaning" by Camille T. Dungy. Published in *What to Eat, What to Drink, What to Leave for Poison* © Red Hen Press, 2006. Reprinted by permission of the author.

"Names" by Bart Edelman. Published in *The Alphabet of Love* © Red Hen Press, 1999. Reprinted by permission of the author.

"Stoops" by Ed Falco. Published in *In the Park of Culture* © The University of Notre Dame Press, 2005. Reprinted by permission of the author.

"The Orange Balloon" by Kate Gale. Published in *Selling the Hammock* © Red Hen Press, 1998. Reprinted by permission of the author.

"Alameda Street" by Douglas Kearney. Published in *Fear, Some* © Red Hen Press, 2006. Reprinted by permission of the author.

"First Grade" by Ron Koertge. Published in *Making Love to Roget's Wife* © The University of Arkansas Press, 1997. Reprinted by permission of the author.

"Girlfriends" by Lisa C. Krueger. Published in *Rebloom* © Red Hen Press, 2004. Reprinted by permission of the author.

"Wolf Leave Tracks Now" by Deena Metzger. Published in *Ruin and Beauty* © Red Hen Press, 2009. Reprinted by permission of the author.

"Marine Band" by Dennis Must. Published in *The MacGuffin* © Schoolcraft College, 2006. Reprinted by permission of the author.

"The Rat" by Miriam Sagan. Published in *Rag Trade* © La Alameda Press, 2004. Reprinted by permission of the author.

"Elephant Story" by Julie Shigekuni. Excerpted from *Unending Nora* © Red Hen Press, 2008. Reprinted by permission of the author.

"Young Boy Dancing at Playa los Muertos" by Peggy Shumaker. Published in *Blaze* © Red Hen Press, 2005. Reprinted by permission of the author.

"The Covenant" by Maurya Simon. Published in *Cartographies* © Red Hen Press, 2008. Reprinted by permission of the author.

"Piano" by Lisa Russ Spaar. Published in *Glass Town* © Red Hen Press, 1999. Reprinted by permission of the author.

"Fish City," from *Everyday Outrages*, published by Red Wind Books, © 1989 by Charles Harper Webb. Reprinted by permission of the author.

"Tehran Treats" by Sholeh Wolpé. Published in *Rooftops of Tehran* © Red Hen Press, 2008. Reprinted by permission of the author.

Contents

Introduction

What do you do when you're the goddess of love, but you don't have any arms? That's the trouble with the Venus de Milo, this crazy armless statue some guy found on an island called Milos about two hundred years back. You've probably seen the statue somewhere before . . . maybe on the cover of this book!

Nobody's quite sure how the Venus de Milo lost her arms. The French sailors who bought her, though, claimed that they battled brigands on a beach to get her. Apparently, her arms were ripped off during the fight!

That's a pretty cool story.

It might not be true, but, now that you've heard that version of the tale, you'll probably never forget it. It's unique and exciting, and only the Venus's own rescuers could have told it like that.

There are an infinite number of Venus de Milos in the world—objects, people, places, and ideas that are strange, cool, and, quite possibly, unique to your life. And, just like those French sailors, you, too, have awesome versions of those Venuses' stories to tell.

Take a look at the prose, poems, and plays the following authors have written. These authors, too, saw Venus de Milos in the world, then told those Venuses' stories like no one ever had before. The sources of the authors' inspirations ranged from the mundane to the insane, and yet all of the stories in this collection were equally worthy of telling because only the stories' own authors could have told them like this.

Why don't you give this writing thing a shot, too? Let this book inspire you to find the Venus de Milos in your life and tell your versions of their stories. It doesn't matter if the stories are true, if they're crazy, or even if they've been told a thousand times before. The important thing is that no one else has told them like you will.

Don't leave your Venuses buried at Milos. Find them and tell their stories—unearth them for the world!

CHARLES HOOD

All My Poems Hate Me

I write poems
but they never come out right—
once I tried to make poetry cupcakes
but all I got was a tray of burned up little nothings,
like a pan filled with twelve tiny black tennis balls.
Another time I had a perfect poem in my head—
it was crazy good, as good as flying an airplane
upside-down at lunchtime over the school—
but when I went to write it down
the words were all whacked and stupid,
bent like old wire in a rusty lot, as if
the paper was drunk and my head was filled
with the noise from a dirty yellow radio
about five blocks away. Another poem
always used to wave at me from the other side
of the window, like I was a fish in the aquarium
and it had a shaker of food and it wasn't going to give me
one speck. One poem became friends with my best friend
and stopped talking to me. One poem caught on fire.
Sometimes I lose my poems. Once one of my poems
tried to email me, but my sister was on the computer
so that was the end of that. I had a really good poem
finished and ready but then I traded it for an iPod
that didn't even work. This one can't remember 5 times 5.
Two of my poems stole from Target and got arrested.
One poem got throw-up on my favorite pants
and MTV never calls to put my poems on tv.

I've got a poem going right now that might be okay—
it has dinosaurs in it, a diamond ring, Jesus, Kobe Bryant,
and six kinds of ice cream. I am writing it on my shoe
so I don't forget the words
and so I can leave a little tiny part of it
pressed down onto all the sidewalks
of the world.

The Author Speaks!

I have published six books of poetry and teach writing at a college, and so sometimes newer writers assume that, for me, or for anybody in this book, writing is easy. Yet we know from the biographies and rough drafts of famous writers that it never is easy for any of us. Sure, once in a while the lightning of inspiration hits the writer right on the head, but, on average, writing is still as hard for me as it is for you. (I have re-written certain pages over 200 times before I figured out how to say what I was trying to say.) Writing can be very frustrating, and this poem admits this "fact hidden in plain sight" right up front. But this poem also tries to say that what you watch on tv or who you talk to at school all can become the material for your next story or poem. Ideas are all around us, starting just with the things we like to see or do. Whacky slang can be a poem, or how you feel when you are happy, or a list of the things that bug you. Not sure how to start? Copy the title of this poem and the first two lines and just go from there, using your own examples. For me, writing just shows how you can hate a thing but love it too, and, as much as writing frustrates me, I still love it with all my heart.

KATE GALE

The Orange Balloon

An orange balloon floats against the sky
let go by a small boy's hand
the hand is unimportant here
it is the balloon on which our happiness depends
or is it the sky?
vast untended full and empty
clouds way too much feeling
but it isn't the sky where our eye rests
it's the small box of blue space
around the orange balloon
the space in which the balloon
moves wallows breathes
this box of blue is your space we say
it defines you
and the clouds drift sideways
the drifting takes years
it takes forever

The Author Speaks!

This is about seeing one image that reminds you of something bigger about your life, someone you love, someone who makes you happy or sad, something that happened to you once. You see the image, and everything comes back to you and holds you for a moment.

Miriam Sagan

The Rat

Our pet hooded rat
Named Mr. Comet
For the star mark on his forehead
Lived in a palatial cage.
We had him trained
To scamper on to our open palms
Grab a peanut, skitter to hide it
In his little house.
He had a rat's hard-scrabble feet,
A feat of engineering tail,
He was so soft, the color of a mink
I loved him, and he liked me, too.

Then one day, someone—
It wasn't me
Left the door ajar—
In came the cat.
By the time we found him
Mr. Comet was clinging terrorized to the bars
So adrenalized he could move
Neither forward nor backward.
Suddenly, his little paws
Gave way and he dropped
Like a ripe plum to the sawdust.
He was uninjured, but obviously in shock,
I was sure he would have
A rat sized heart attack.

My daughter wept, turned out the lights
Sat with Mr. Comet in the dark,
Told him he would be alright.

I was surprised, but the child's knowledge
Proved correct,
By the next morning
He scampered as ever
Whiskers a-quiver
Up one of my shoulders
And down the next.
He seems happy, to this day;
Still, I can't help but wonder
If his rat soul awoke to the existence of danger
He who had been raised
Without reference to predator or prey,
Petted, hand fed,
Suddenly seeing his natural enemy.
And the cat?
She seemed different at first
Obviously top of the food chain
Designed for one thing.
But soon that faded too,
She purred in my lap,
I was the only creature here
Who wasn't natural in the habitat
Who kept wanting

To make meaning of what had happened
To all of us
To cat, rat, child, and me—
To tell the story.

The Author Speaks!

I wrote this poem as it actually happened at my house. My daughter had a lot of pets at this time. I didn't include the guinea pigs because I wanted the poem to focus on the basic story and conflict. The poem is narrative in form, that is, what moves it forward is the telling of a story. It uses very partial rhyme, just at the end, to emphasize the sense of conclusion.

Ron Koertge

First Grade

Until then, every forest
had wolves in it, we thought
it would be fun to wear snowshoes
all the time, and we could talk to water.

So who is this woman with the gray
breath calling out names and pointing
to the little desks we will occupy
for the rest of our lives?

The Author Speaks!

I tend to write about the things around me. I was visiting a middle school to talk about one of my Young Adult novels and glanced into a first grade classroom. Some people think school in general is where imagination and creativity is siphoned out of kids, so this poem would be right up their alley. What I think about school doesn't matter. I wanted to write a good poem.

GAYLORD BREWER

Being Lon Chaney, Jr.

No ankle manacled to bedpost,
although hair swoops away and eyes
twitch with terrible revelation.

The sun is sinking (*the sun is sinking!*)
behind breezes like Bavarian streams
cooling an unlucky man's hot flesh.

Thank God that innocent girl, innkeeper's
daughter, escorts the Baron tonight.
Let the carnival run late, let no one return
while the moon hums its bloated anthem.

You tremble like an animal startled
in its skin, shoulders hunched, teeth
beginning to grow as the whole dark world,
even Gypsy wagons, tense to see what
you'll do next, you and your sweet curse.

The Author Speaks!

Which movie monster is your favorite? Dracula? King Kong? Frankenstein's monster? What kinds of feelings do you have for these characters and for how society treats them? During the day, the Wolf Man was a nice guy named Larry Talbot. He didn't want to be a monster every time the full moon rose, but he had this thing inside him he couldn't control. I always felt sorry for Talbot, and I was always happy when the old Gypsy woman cared for him and understood his pain. On the other hand, Dracula always seemed to really *like* being Count Dracula. But King Kong never would have hurt anybody if we'd just left him alone in his jungle, right? Lon Chaney, Jr. was the actor who played the Wolf Man in a couple of the classics. He was cool. (His dad was cool, too, and played the Hunchback of Notre Dame. Crazy family!) What creature would you play in the movies? Write a poem really getting into what makes your monster tick. How do feel about it all, blessing or curse? And in your movie/poem, how do people feel about *you*?

Maurya Simon

The Covenant

Beneath the pines' dark thatch of shadow
bleeds an incidental leak of light
through which a blur of fur speeds by:
a gloss of rump, the spongy, rumpled thud
of moss pressed underfoot, then silence
catches in my ears—we meet, the deer
and I, head-on: me with my halo of gnats,
he with his rack of antlers held aloft.
Steam from our velvet nostrils mingles;
our eyes bulge huge with awe, our lips
part voicelessly, then thunder rocks the air,
and he is gone. A bird ruptures into song.

The Author Speaks!

I was hiking alone one day, in the San Gabriel Mountains in Southern California, when I encountered a male deer (also known as a buck). I had been lost in my own thoughts, barely even noticing my surroundings and looking down at the trail, when I was surprised to look up suddenly and see this deer staring at me. He was only a few feet in front of me, and he was equally surprised to see me!

When writing this poem, I wanted to try to capture that moment of two animal species being startled by each other at the same time. I also wanted to convey the silent agreement, or "covenant," that we each made, recognizing each other's right to be on the trail and in the world. I tried to write a long first sentence using a structure that I'd never before used in a poem. So the poem's first sentence is made up of eight lines that wind through the poem, adding on images like pearls being strung on a string for a necklace. Finally, I wanted to add "sound effects" to the poem, too, so that the silence that occurs—when I meet up with the deer—would seem as "loud" as the sound I heard earlier of the deer's hooves walking on the forest trail.

Camille T. Dungy

Cleaning

I learned regret at Mother's sink,
jarred tomatoes, river-mud brown,
a generation old, lumping
down the drain. Hating wasted space,
I had discarded what I could
not understand. I hadn't known
a woman to fight drought or frost
for the promise of winter meals,
hadn't known my great-grandmother,
or what it was to have then lose
the company of that woman
who, upon seeing her namesake,
child of her child, grown and gliding
into marriage, gifted the fruit
of her garden, a hard-won strike
against want. Opening the jar,
I knew nothing of the rotting
effect, the twisting grip of years
spent packing, of years spent moving,
further each time, from known comforts:
a grandmother's garden, her rows
always neat, the harvest: bright wealth
Mother hoarded. I understood
only the danger of a date
so old. Understanding clearly
what is fatal to the body,
I only understood too late
what can be fatal to the heart.

The Author Speaks!

Have you ever thought you were doing something to help and realized after the fact that you hurt someone instead? This poem is about that sort of act. The speaker tries to clean her mother's cupboards and ends up throwing away a jar of stewed tomatoes that had been a wedding gift from her mother's own grandmother. The poem speaks of the regret the speaker experiences, the connection between the mother and her grandmother, and the many ways women find to demonstrate love.

ELIZABETH BRADFIELD

Maid of Honor

Aqua rustle of taffeta over flattop, foreign
zipper up her spine, all up her spine,
from coccyx to nape, her un-
willowy arms in puffed sleeves,
and her mother's voice muffled but
clear: *For me, then. Wear it for me.*
It's your sister's wedding.

There's a photograph I have of her at nine
in Florida, standing by the mechanical elephant
at Pedro's mini-golf, quarter in her pocket for the ride,
one eye squint-shut, one hand in the hip-cocked
pocket of her jeans. Tomboy in a blazer
that her mother must have chosen
with her, bought for her, approved back then.

May of 1968. Palm trees flagging over astro-turf.
Yes, I think, each time I look at it, *how could anyone*
miss what she was becoming? And yes, she should
be able to straddle that elephant, sit in the red saddle
as her parents smile and wave and the upraised
trunk blows luck all over her.

She pulls up to the church on a Nighthawk,
the only vehicle she owns, swings her leg
to the ground, underskirts rustling down
over black boots. And now it's clear

to her mother on the church steps
holding the bouquet for her other daughter. It's clear
that even pumps and hose, a manicure, a waxing and,
for god's sake, some makeup, even the desire
that brought her here to *Try, for me*
couldn't make her that kind
of ordinary.

The Author Speaks!

First, let me say that almost no one on the planet looks good or "normal" in a brides-maid's dress. Lined up as a group, all those different bodies in the same outfit they probably had no voice in choosing, someone's going to look out of place.

This poem is part of a group of poems I've written about women who don't look "feminine" and how they are perceived. I want, in these poems, to praise a different kind of beauty and to explore how a beauty outside of the "ordinary" might be appreciated.

For me, this is a love poem. It is a poem about familial love, about the dress-wearer's willingness to put on something that she knows will make her look ridiculous because it will make her mother happy. Then, in turn, it's a poem about how a mother who wants her daughter to look "normal" comes to a point when she can no longer ignore what's obvious: her daughter is different from whatever expectations the mother had. The speaker of the poem, the poet telling the story, is clearly fond of the dress-wearer and clearly thinks she has a beauty of her own.

What makes us beautiful? Maybe it's love—being loved for our own particular and unique selves.

Note: A Nighthawk is a type of motorcycle, and the "she" is wearing boots under that dress not to be defiant, but because you really can't drive a motorcycle in high heels. It's just not safe.

SHOLEH WOLPÉ

Tehran Treats

Every day on your way home from school,
you beg your mother for treats.
Hot beets, potatoes roasted on red coals, crunchy
raw almonds, green plums so sour they bite into teeth.

The banana vendor is old, yellow, bent
and not once do you ask your mother
why his children pick up and lick the banana skins
you carelessly throw into the straw basket by his cart.

The Author Speaks!

Do you know where Tehran is? Find it on the map. It is the capital of Iran. Iran is located in the Middle East. We always hear about the politics of other countries and all the bad things governments and the extremist groups do and we forget that ordinary people live ordinary lives in these countries. The beauty of literature is that we get to hear about the real people living in these countries. Literature helps us learn about one another's cultures and see that, in the end, we are all human beings trying to live happy and fulfilled lives. Another thing literature helps us understand is that some of the fundamental problems in our societies are almost the same. Humanity is like a tree that gives many kinds of fruit, but the roots of the tree are the same for everyone.

What can you learn from this poem, "Tehran Treats"? It's a very short poem, but if you read it several times you will begin to learn a great deal about the child in the poem and that even though he or she lives in Tehran, you have a lot in common with him or her:

1. The child goes to school every day.
2. He or she begs for treats after school.
3. The snacks enumerated in the poem are not like the ones you get in the U.S. This teaches you a little bit about what children love to eat in Tehran.
4. Bananas in Tehran are a real treat, so the child's mother often treats her child to bananas.
5. The bananas are sold from a cart like ice cream is sold from a cart in the U.S.
6. The child notices the age and sickliness of the vendor. She or he also notices that the vendor's children are always with him.
7. The child notices that the vendor's children lick the banana skins she or he throws in the cart. Does she know why they are doing that? Can't they ask their father for a banana?

8. Why doesn't the child ask his or her mother the reason for this? Could it be that the child already knows that the banana vendor is so poor that he cannot afford to give his own children the exotic fruit? That he must sell his fruit in order to be able to buy bread for his family?

9. Have you yourself ever done that? Have you seen children of privileged families who behave that way?

Sometimes, when we see poverty, we ignore it because we either feel helpless to do something about it or we have learned to not care. Even though this poem takes place in Tehran, it could be a poem about a child from a wealthy family in Los Angeles, San Francisco, or London.

The poem draws you in by using "you" instead of "I" or "he" or "she." This way you are in the story—you become that child.

ED FALCO

Stoops

Not smooth surfaced ones like brownstones in better neighborhoods, but blond and rough-textured, with stones embedded. I could run my finger over a stone, the surface smooth, but only an instant before the ripping texture of concrete, ragged and sharp. Crisp angles perfect for the pink Spaldene to bounce back, high edge shot like a home run, kids cheering run! run! run! Or wooden stoops like bunk beds we'd lie down on when we were tired. Kids. Brooklyn. We'd jump off, climbing one step higher each time, until from the top step you could feel it in your spine. It might make the back of your head hurt. Where were our parents? I can't remember a parent ever to say stop. We jumped handrails to slate or concrete sidewalk on dares. We catapulted cast-iron spear-picket fences. We shinned up lampposts and hung off the top over traffic. Summers we ran the streets morning to dark, climbing barbed wire, crossing alleys, crawling through any opening. Only at night the mothers' voices like solitary bird calls, your name singing along the darkening streets.

The Author Speaks!

"Stoops" is largely about the rhythm of the language, the way the sound of the sentences evokes a sense of childhood and children at play. Most of this short fiction presents a child's perspective on stoops. A stoop, to a child, is not a utilitarian construction meant to facilitate entry to a building. To a child, a stoop is something to sit on, play on, jump off. The children in this particular piece are in Brooklyn, New York, where kids play stoopball, a game in which the "batter" throws a rubber ball (a pink Spalene, when the writer was a kid) at a stoop, with the object of having it bounce back to the street, where the "fielder" is waiting. If he or she catches the ball, it's an out. If the ball bounces on the street, it's a hit. After that, the rules vary from stoop to stoop, city to city. The memory of stoops in this short fiction leads to other city-kid memories, including lots of play that is inherently dangerous, including climbing, running, and crawling into places kids would be wiser to avoid. "Stoops" ends with an image most kids raised in a city can relate to—the sound of a mother's voice calling them back to home and safety.

"Stoops" doesn't need to be explained. It's a short fiction about city kids at play. What city kid doesn't recognize the final image: a mother's voice calling him or her home?

BART EDELMAN

Names

Say your name twice,
Repeating each syllable
Softly and slowly, at first,
As if the world would be
A lonely space without it;
Ask yourself why
You were given this name
And trace it
On the back of a leaf,
Or down the edge of a stem,
Touching every letter
With the tip of your tongue.
Now, wonder aloud
What you would lose
And who you would be
If this familiar name
No longer belonged to you
And was bartered away
On the price of a song.
For when life seems too busy
With people and places and things
That make you question
Why you are here,
Then write your name
In the warm rain
The night left behind,
And always know

It will be waiting
To follow you home.

The Author Speaks!

I am always fascinated by people's names and how these names often define Individuals. How much do names tell us about people and the lives they live? Some people love their names, others spend a lifetime attempting to forget their names, and I imagine there are even others who haven't thought that much about the names they were given at birth.

Early in a child's development a sense of identity usually comes from a name and what it projects about the person to the rest of the world. Countless numbers of people make a very bold statement by either changing their names legally or selecting another name for themselves by which they are called, depending upon personal or business situations. Other people choose to carry "nicknames" into adulthood. Finally, how many of us were named for another person, and what does that contribute to our sense of identity and purpose in life? Try discussing the significance of your own name and those of family members or friends closest to you.

Questions:
1. What does your name mean to you?
2. Who gave you your name and what is its significance?
3. Do you like your name?
4. If you changed your name, what would you change it to? Why?
5. Does society associate people with certain names? Do you do the same?
6. Are there names you like? Dislike?
7. How does a distinct name define us?
8. In the poem "Names," why "Say your name twice"?
9. Why touch "every letter with the tip of your tongue"?
10. What is the meaning of the word "bartered"?
11. Why does your name "follow you home"?

Erinn Batykefer

Eureka Vacuum

Little girl opens the coat-closet door
and stares down the sleeping vacuum,
harmless beneath the fancy coats, its whipcord
wrapped up, spy-lamp eye shut off. Still, her bones
rattle in her skin the way the china clatters
in the china closet when the vacuum rumbles past.
Under her mother's hand, the thing sweeps corners
with its cycloptic eye, its searchlight gaze cast
under all the chairs and beds—the name says it all:
EUREKA emblazoned across the vacuum's blunt
red nose. It's a way to find things out and when it's on,
there's nowhere to hide a bit of dirt, no safe place for a secret.
Tomorrow, her mother will coast around in its wake,
seeing everything it sees as she cleans up the place.

The Author Speaks!

This poem was one in a series of sonnets I wrote that I referred to as "The Creepy Childhood Sonnets." I was trying to explore the difference between how we see things as children and how we see things as adults. In exploring the vacuum in "Eureka Vacuum," I realized that the little girl's fear of the vacuum had much less to do with the vacuum itself, or the noise it made, but was more metaphorical: the nerve-jangling sensations she experiences when the vacuum is on is a metaphor for how she feels about her mother finding out her secrets, or wanting to. The real fear of the poem is not the little girl's fear of the vacuum itself, which she will grow out of, but fear of nothing being private or secret.

Douglas Kearney

Alameda Street

for Deshawn, Eric, Dallas, Jerome & Lerone

We brown boys
    play
        stick games,
   say
        nicknames
like Big D, Evil E;
and conjure Knievel
with jigsawed dirt bikes
and sewer curbs
for asphalt launch pads.
    We all sweat
    to know flight
    for just
    a minute.

We brown boys,
    hair
        all knaps,
   wear
        ballcaps'
broken brims. Broken rims
from hungry slamdunks,
pro-ball pipe dreams
over ice cream man's
"Pop Goes the Weasel."

We all hunt
change from cords',
Bermudas
and mamas.

We brown boys—
　　smack
　　　　　talking
　　slap
　　　　　boxing—
stay bragging and bagging,
drinking summer from hoses
and water bomb barrages.
We throw rocks at garages
making no dents.
　　We all just
　　trying to leave
　　a mark.

The Author Speaks!

I wrote "Alameda Street" as a kind of ode to the guys I grew up with about fifteen miles from downtown Los Angeles in Altadena. I grew up listening to rap music and it's a tradition in rap to name folks from your block. This poem gave me a chance to do that.

I wanted "Alameda Street" to have an innocent, simple sound to contrast with the growing tension many of us felt as we passed from childhood into our late teens. I was the youngest, my brother Dallas was four years older than I, and Deshawn was the oldest, several years older than my brother—so we were dealing with different expectations even as we hung out and played on the same street we had always been on.

Oh!—"Knievel" is a reference to Evel Knievel, an extreme sports motorcyclist from back in the day. He used to jump his motorcycle over long lines of cars, through rings of fire, from cliffs, etc. There are other references—Bermudas, cords, and bagging (the first two refer to shorts and corduroys, "bagging" means to insult each other playfully).

Peggy Shumaker

Young Boy Dancing at Playa los Muertos

Had he been naked
as he skipped
shivering
out of the waves
we would not have known
he was so poor.

But he was not
naked. He wore
around his hips
an exhausted
pair of cast-off
underwear
gathered up at the hip,
secured
with the wire twist
from some tourist's
loaf of bread.

He shivered,
the edges of his lips
blue as the Virgin's veil.
Semana Santa, Holy Week, too early
really for perfect swimming.
Vendors hawked
Taxco silver, mangoes
on a stick, onyx seahorses

chiming, whole perch
skewered and seared.
His eyes swam after
the fish boy.

Timbales called out the guitarrón—
mariachis knocked Norteño beats
blanket to blanket up the beach.
The skinny one held on to his saggy
pants, elbowed close to sing along.
Someone else's fat papá lifted an eyebrow
in invitation, laughed, and together
man and boy danced a slick merengue,
flicked their hips ta-ta-ta,
swirled, one hand
suave against the belly,
the other a green rooster
kikiriki-ki
sunrise all day long!

The boy's whole body
told its truth—
he was not starving, no matter
what his ribs said. And his skin
could go ahead and offer the opinions
of its array of scars—no slash,
no welt, no still-healing burn

along his face, neck, shoulder
could talk louder
than the genius of his tiny
hips, those quick and playful
acts of God.

The Author Speaks!

This poem takes place on a beach in Mexico. I watched a very young, very hungry young boy dancing. His exuberance and his suffering were both apparent.

Try a poem of your own that takes place in a location that matters to you, one that you can see clearly. Focus on a character in action. Show us one precise moment. For extra credit, use words from more than one language and rhythms from something in the scene (in my poem I used the music).

SHELLEY SAVREN

Talking with Her Fingers

My grandmother mashes salmon
into patties, drops them into sizzling oil
then smacks her fingers one by one,

anticipating the pureed texture, nostrils
on alert. Each finger enters that opening
in queue as she sucks raw mixture

then pulls out—fast. She needs that forefinger
clean for scolding. I can't eat, watching it
wag at me across the table. She orders me

around the kitchen. Boil chicken, slice garlic,
onion—not so thin—chop celery, carrots,
add pepper, salt—not too much. I like her

better before the black and white TV
in an ironed housedress with yarn wrapped
around her forefinger as she crochets

quickly, afghans for everybody's bed
or at breakfast cooling my farina with milk.
Before I leave for school I sneak lemons

from the frig and as I hurry from her house
I bite the skin, squeeze juice across my fingers
to cover up the stinky smells that stay there.

The Author Speaks!

Think of a family member and a time that you spent with him or her. Use one or two of your five senses to describe that event. For example, if you were in a garage with your grandfather working on a car, what did the oil feel like on your hands? If you were in the kitchen with your mom, what smells were there? Describe the interaction between you and the family member. How did you feel about that person? How did you feel about the way she or he was treating you? Don't just state the feeling, though. Let the reader discover it through your descriptions.

Lisa C. Krueger

Girlfriends

I put lotion on her hands,
Let's try to relax, she does
at home but not in the schoolyard
where girls already know who has a fat butt
and who is going to be the most popular person totally
for the rest of her life. She is six.
Her friends are six and seven.
She calls them friends, I call them
classmates. She cannot
bear to see the difference.
Six years old. Why should she?

At night in the bath
she gazes at wet plumpness,
pleads with me *Am I fat?*
You are not. You are six and lovely, I say.
But the girls have told her, they
have given her a name, a title, a crown,
they put it on her
and because they are her friends,
she wears it.

The Author Speaks!

This poem is about two sets of friendships: the relationship between a mother and her daughter and the relationship between a girl and her friends. The mother in this poem is trying to be supportive, while the girlfriends don't seem to be. This poem raises questions about the meaning of friendship, and about competition between friends.

The poem also addresses the topic of how people see themselves. At the end of the poem, the girl in the tub wears the name "fat" like it's a "crown" because the label is from her "friends." Hopefully this poem makes the reader think about the power classmates can have over each other, and the meaning of friendship.

Frances Payne Adler

Invention

for Molly and Mike

I wish you love, the bright kind, the filled with light kind, the
beside you in the night kind, the side-splitting laughter upside-
down ferris wheel ride kind, and the wide kind, the expandable
elasticized durable tough as hide, work out the rough times kind

I wish you words, the dear kind, the have no fear kind, the I'll
always love you kind, the clear kind, the I hear you kind, the
we're different and don't always have to agree, supporting
each other to grow kind

I wish you health, the working up a sweat running to the
breadstore kind, the organic food kind, the tall tree clean air
kind, the ball's in the air, gimme a break, tearing
down the stress, music is a must kind

I wish you kids, the wealthy in health kind, the such a
cute toosh kind, the gritty hands from sands at the beach,
singing at the table, arms around your neck, strong
as a trans-Atlantic cable kind

the Sunday morning lolling in bed kind, the redhot chili
bumping car willies, all day long sillies, dollies and bikes,
lollies and Nikes, and years and years and years of the
I remember when I was a kid kind

I wish you vision, the let's re-create marriage kind, the let's re-imagine the institution from scratch kind, the loosed from its moorings, no more obscuring handed-down versions kind, the turn of the twenty-first century, you've got all you need to invent the exponentury Molly and Mike kind

The Author Speaks!

My son asked me to write a poem for his wedding. I was honored, and plenty intimidated. So I created for myself the fun of writing in a new form, one that I made up. Yes, there are sonnets and villanelles and haiku and sestinas. None of these. I wanted something fresh. So here's the form I set for myself: I could work on writing the poem solely when I was happy. Really happy. You know, the heightened kind that comes fleetingly. I wanted to weave "happy" into the poem without ever using the word. It was the feeling of it that I wanted to come through in the poem. Some poems struggle into being. This one slipped out in five hours. I wrote it while flying across the country returning from a great trip, 30,000 feet up in the air. And if you listen closely, you can hear, within it, the music of the clouds.

Have you ever wanted to write a poem for someone's birthday or anniversary or wedding? Or has someone ever asked you to write one for them? It can be a challenge, and it can also be great fun.

LISA RUSS SPAAR

Piano

for Donald Justice

Red quince branch,
curved and oriental,
drops blossoms
on the black shoulders of a piano.
Black ship, burial box:
inside, slaves chained together
shift their bracelets and moan;
the felted hammers wait
asleep as weights in a clock.

At the end of a long hallway,
steps.
Hands rise from a lap.
Light strikes the face of the sleeper.

The Author Speaks!

This poem is a kind of "definition" or riddle poem. It begins by describing a cultured, almost romanticized still life scene in which a flowering branch is depicted atop a piano. The scene is fairly literal, descriptive, and realistic. The dropped petals, however, introduce a note of decay, of time passing, and the piano itself is said to have "shoulders." Through this comparison to a human body, the piano is personified, and right away we know that the poem is going to be more than just a *literal* poem about an object; it is going to be figurative: the piano is going to represent or suggest something connected to but also more than or beyond itself. In the lines that follow, the piano is compared, through metaphor, to a black ship, and then to a coffin ("burial box"). In what ways might a ship be seen as a coffin? Under what circumstances? The wire-wrapped strings found inside a grand piano are, in the next lines, compared to "slaves," and the reader recalls ships that held human beings in their bellies, carrying them across oceans into death-like lives of servitude. The hammers of the piano keys, which must strike these wires in order to produce sound, are then compared to the weights of a clock. All of these images suggest arrested time, capture, poised silence, suspense, waiting: the moments before music, and the human story inside all song, all art.

The stanza break signals that something is about to happen. What follows is almost like a scene from a movie. Instead of being "inside" the piano, the camera angle is now somewhere outside the piano. We hear steps. Hands rise from a lap. It is as though someone has approached the piano and has seated him or herself before it. When the poem says "Light strikes the face of the sleeper," the reader wakes from the dream-like language in stanza one. She or he realizes that the piano has also been awakened into music, into life, and that this music grows out of the decay and pain and waiting that have been described in the first part of the poem. Jazz, for example, and the blues are types of music that grew very specifically out of the wrongful capture and enforced silence of African slaves. Such music sometimes comes to us from a long way off in terms of time, place, and experience. In this way, we see that a piano is more than just a piano; history and human beings make music out of time and experience. In a way, the piano is like a poem—it requires the reader to bring it to life.

Deena Metzger

Wolf Leave Tracks Now

The animal looking out of the bars
is relieved to know she is an animal
but nevertheless they have put her
behind bars,
when they look at her through bars
they become the bars, so to speak,
look how they spread themselves out
between the dark poles.
She does not want to be those bars
but she is behind them nevertheless,
she is pleased she is an animal
but she also knows
she is behind bars,
she
who would not know
how to construct bars,
she is an animal,
that is what she knows,
she is the animal
that is
what she knows,

and she knows
the animal,
she knows.

The Author Speaks!

In order to understand the poem, you have to be in the poem. You have to be the animal that the poem speaks about, in prison, looking out through the bars at the people who are gazing at you. The poem asks you to see what it is like to be in a zoo. It emphasizes the difference between the animal and the observer and asks the reader to consider that the animal is probably a kinder being who would never treat the observer the way the observer is treating the animal.

When I wrote the poem, zoos were considered a great cultural and educational institution. That was when zoos competed with each other for animals and developed reputations for how many exotic animals they could acquire. That was before we were awakened to environmental devastation and species decline.

When I wrote the poem in the 70s there were also too many people in prison. Now there are far, far too many people in prison. It is not sufficient to say that we treat people like animals. The poem asks us to consider how cruelly we treat animals and people and asks us to observe ourselves and reflect on our own behavior. People are studying the animal, but the animal is studying us.

Finally, the poem allies with the animal not as a victim but as someone who knows more than the observer, the zoo keeper or the warden. The animal and the prisoner are seen as beings who carry intelligence and great sensitivity.

The purpose of poetry is to help us see the world in entirely new ways. Poetry turns everything we think we know upside down. It gives us new eyes.

CHARLES HARPER WEBB

Fish City

We lived in the country until I was six
with a woods behind our house
and, twenty yards in, Fish Creek.
I'd fall asleep lulled by its gurgle and swish.

An hour there was more fun than a week
most places. Bullfrogs, turtles, tadpoles
splashed and wriggled everywhere.
And lizards, garter snakes, and schools

of punkinseeds: blue, green, and red,
scrappy little guys glad for a fat worm
hung from a cane pole. They lived in Fish
City I used to say, each family in its own

fish house, like Dutch houses in books.
They had fish gardens with fish tulips,
fish streets, fish cars, fish garbage trucks.
We were best friends, playing, telling

jokes, having birthday parties all the time.
When I caught one I let him go; or if not,
Mom fried him up, I wouldn't waste a bite,
and next day he'd swim home as good as new.

I can still see them on the day I moved,
standing in their fish doorways,

the eaten ones there with the rest, all crying,
waving me goodbye.

The Author Speaks

This poem tries to re-create the world of an imaginative six-year-old. The child makes a magical place of the creek behind his house, imagining that the fish live much like people he's seen in books about Holland.

It may be that the child is lonely, so he creates friends of his own. In any case, he doesn't share Fish City; there is no mention of anyone else joining him there.

The child has to face one big moral problem: sometimes he eats his friends. His solution is the same one found by indigenous people from many cultures. If the food animal is respected and not wasted, the child decides, it will die willingly, and return to earth as good as new.

The last stanza is an example of what psychologists call "projection." The fish do what the child wants to do (and, quite possibly, does). They cry and wave goodbye to the friend who is leaving them, not just to live in another town, but another world—the world of big kids, where his fish friends know they won't be welcome, and can't go.

Sebastian Matthews

For an Hour Mickey Mouse

There's a sidewalk in Ann Arbor
where a joker has painted the famous set of ears.

You don't know at first what you're looking at
until, at some exact point of summer afternoon,

the sun comes down off its sundial arc
and a parking meter shadow rises up its slender stalk.

And for an hour Mickey Mouse comes alive
in the bored gaze of walkers.

The Author Speaks!

"For an Hour Mickey Mouse" is a straight-forward poem with a simple goal: to get the reader to see what the walker witnesses when unexpectedly faced with this "Mickey" street art. But first I must give the reader some context, so I tell them that "some joker" has painted Mickey's famous ears on the sidewalk. Separated from the rest of the cartoon character, the ears are not recognizable, for it's not until the shadow of an old-fashioned parking meter rises up to connect with the ears that the image come to life in the walker's/reader's mind.

The main technique I use in this poem is metaphor. When a poet describes one thing (a parking meter) as another (a flower), he is making a metaphoric connection. Sometimes the poet can be direct about this connection ("Love is a rose"), and sometimes he can imply the connection. When I compare a parking meter pole to a plant stalk, I am suggesting that the meter is much like a flower responding to the sun.

The bigger metaphor in this poem, of course, is the sundial. I say the sun comes down its "sundial arc." It's not a big leap on my part. The way a sundial tells time by recording the passing of the sun is the same basic experience the street artist is employing for his visual magic trick.

I often use real life experience for subject matter in my poems. I wrote this poem soon after witnessing Mickey's coming to life before my eyes. I do this for a few reasons. First, it makes me pay attention in my daily life. Poems don't always spring from the mind, or from the poet's pen as he or she sits at the desk. They can come from anywhere, spurred by almost anything. Even the metaphors I turned to—the sundial, the flower—come out of the truth of the experience.

Ron Carlson

The Proper Wolf

Why not start the story at the high point, the character trembling and the door about to open? That's where we are now with the wolf in the bed, dressed in a pink patterned nightgown, the cotton thick and soft and the embroidered throat tender on his hairy neck. The sleep bonnet rakishly askew, earwise, but tied chastely under his chin in the coarse wolf hair there. The lamp is low, and he leans back under the heavy quilt, feeling his wolf's heart pounding him deeper in the covers. He is about to discover whether his costume will work.

He wasn't always like this, though his history has its own curiosity. You'd think such a one was raised by humans in a paneled game room in the suburbs eating soy milk and mixed nuts, but no. He was a wolf from deep in the woods, the densest part of the forest where little light falls. At night when he was a cub, he could hear the distant pounding of the blades of machines as the world cut closer into the wilderness, and he felt himself drawn to the edge of the woods where he could see the men working. He saw their boots and their hard hats, and he was filled with wonder. Well, wonder is an imprecise feeling, though powerful, and part of it was a driving curiosity which he could not control.

Who were these creatures? What were they doing? How did they make lights at night?

He wandered out into the margin, past the cut trees onto the bladed surface, and he was surprised that they saw him, pointed at him, alarmed, and that someone shot a gun in his direction. It happened every time he tried to go see. He could not control his curiosity and every time he left the trees, some man shot at him.

The advice he received from his family and from the other wolves was conventional advice, and it was hard for him to apply. They said, "Stay away from men and their doings." He listened, but he knew he could not. He was powerless before his burning curiosity. He'd seen the lights at night, the square windows in the homes, and the blinking lights from the little shops on the corners.

His first costume was a flannel shirt and a handkerchief he dragged from a clothes-line late one afternoon. In the dark of the woods he struggled to get the shirt on. He rolled in it until it went on, and then he spent four hours buttoning it with his teeth. He was determined and patient. He waited a day for a pair of khakis to appear on the line, legs spread in the sun, and he measured it carefully and jumped into those pants. The feeling he carried in his beating wolf heart as he walked through the village that afternoon was the feeling he'd been wanting. On two legs, with his paws in his pockets, he made one tour, past the post office and the drugstore, his reflection looking like a man, mostly, and when he loped to the thicket and lay in the underbrush, he knew the way his life had turned.

The closet in his den thickened with clothing of all sorts: skirts, pants, dresses, polo shirts by Ralph Lauren, turtlenecks, college sweatshirts, baseball caps, capes, Capri pants, gym socks, argyle socks, sandals, cowboy boots, penny loafers and pajamas. He spent hours preparing and would go into town and ride the bus back and forth, a newspaper clipped under his arm.

He was careful not to smile, but kept his head down, while his heart crashed around like a box full of rocks. He drank coffee in the red booth at the diner and he had his shoes repaired at Tim's Leather Fix-it. He became adept at buttons, zippers, catches of all kinds including those in the back. He developed some tastes and understood he looked best in grays and blacks, and he took all his pastel T-shirts and one beautiful pink oxford cloth dress shirt to the Thrift Store. He learned to tie a Windsor knot and found two herringbone vests.

He came to know he could not control this either. He needed to dress to go out. He no longer roamed the woods at night, a trail of saliva in the corner of his mouth. Now he carried a handkerchief and was careful not to drool. Some nights, he had nowhere to go, but he had to dress up. He met some ridicule from the other wolves, but it diminished as he learned to dress better and better.

About this time, he began to see the girl. Everyone knew the forest path and some people used it regularly: the joggers, the thieves, the woodsmen, and the girl. She was more than a girl, though to call her a woman would have stretched it. She wore the red cape which had a hood which sometimes she wore up and sometimes she wore down. He envied her, that cape. His own cape made him appear too severe and when he wore it into the village, children avoided him. Her cape was the only red thing he'd ever seen.

He began to follow her. He knew he would. He followed everyone: the joggers and their smell of sweat and soap, the thieves and their wake of vulgar mumbling, the woodsman and his floating trail of sawdust and the glint of his axe. When she went into her grandmother's cottage at the edge of the village, he listened at the door and heard their conversation. The two talked about the girl's mother, worried about the men she was now seeing. She was dating the owner of the Laundromat, a man the wolf knew because he took clothing from that place weekly. The wolf liked the man because the man was cautious and when the wolf was there opening the dryers, the man turned right back around and went into his office. He was a sweet, careful man with thinning hair.

When the two women, the girl and her grandmother, talked there was an air of sarcasm about it all, as if they were superior to the others in their stories, and this feeling bothered the wolf. He then heard something that hurt his wolf's heart. The girl said something like, it's almost as bad as that old wolf who goes around in clothing, and then the women laughed: ha ha ha ha ha ha.

It was a hard moment for the wolf to hear this news. He had fooled no one, and was himself, as a wolf, a fool. He hung his head down. He looked at the brown gabardine suit he was wearing and the shined ankle high dress shoes. Oh, he was sick in his heart in a second, and he fled that place.

Wearing nothing but a rueful smile, the wolf returned the clothing he had taken from the village. He ran back and forth from his den to the Laundromat and to other locations he had visited. It felt good to run, but he wasn't thinking. He wanted to empty his den and leave that country behind. When he was taking a bundle of summer things back to the laundry, he heard the owner and the girl's mother talking. It was bad news: the grandmother was gravely ill. They had to keep the news from the girl until she passed her exams at school.

The next day he saw the girl running on the woodland path, her red hooded cape aflutter. The wolf had returned all of his garments, and he was lying in a bush. He saw her face, the worry there, and her face was like a lesson to him.

In a second he was on all fours streaking toward the grandmother's cottage. He ran like the wind when it is a fast wind which knows where it is going, and he leaped through the bedroom window and burrowed into the grandma's nightgown in a second. Tying the bonnet was nothing. And suddenly he was in the bed.

Now we are at the moment. The door opened carefully and the face of the girl, shined by the tears, appeared. "Grandma," she said. "Are you sick?"

"No," the wolf answered. "Do I look sick? I'm a little tired, but that's why I have this bed. This bed will sleep me up, and we'll go dancing tomorrow."

"Oh, grandma, really? They told me you were sick and that I might not see you again."

"Well, can you see me?"

"Oh, yes," said the girl, and she hugged the wolf, her head on his chest, sobbing.

"How are your exams at school?" the wolf asked.

"Oh, they're just fine. I'll pass easily. But you know what we were talking about the other day?"

"What?"

"The wolf? You know my dear wolf and his clothing?"

The wolf now felt his heart stop and park itself against a rib, hiding.

"Yes," he said.

"Oh grandma, he's gone! I haven't seen him in an age. I miss him so. He was the only interesting thing about this village. I wanted to meet him. I want to write his story and find out his name and where he gets his jackets."

The wolf's heart was a wolf's heart filled with happiness. He considered what to say and then said, "They looked like the mayor's jackets to me. And that wolf, my dear, don't worry; he'll be back. He's probably shopping right now."

The Author Speaks!

Questions:
1. This is a retelling of a fairy tale. Which one?
2. What is the story of Little Red Riding Hood?
3. What is the major difference between "The Proper Wolf" and the tale of Little Red Riding Hood?
4. Why is this story called "The Proper Wolf?"
5. How would you describe the character of the wolf in this story?
6. What is the biggest surprise in the story?
7. Why does the story start where it starts?
8. Would you say that this story has a happy ending?
9. Can you think of a fairy tale that you would like to retell?

DENNIS MUST

Marine Band

Chester Grange joined the Marines.

He left his harmonicas at home. Mrs. Grange displayed the prized collection on the fireplace mantel under her son's portrait. When Mother and I would visit, she'd place one of the instruments in my hand. "Please don't try to play it, Jimmy. Chester's breath is still inside its reeds. Mustn't let it escape till he returns from parachuting behind enemy lines. Then I'll bet he'll let you have one of 'em." The women stayed close by, eyeing me periodically while they conversed to make certain I didn't put the harp to my lips.

A service flag with one blue star graced her living room window. Several gold stars hung in the neighbors' windows.

One afternoon, Mrs. Grange handed me Chester's enormous chromatic harmonica. When she and my mother disappeared briefly into the kitchen for tea, I lifted it to my nose trying to whiff Chester's breath in the blowholes. It smelled like Chiclets.

I was in the fifth grade then, and Chester, like other young men in my hometown, was fighting the "Krauts" as Mrs. Grange always reminded us. Mother would sit across from her quietly inquiring of the comely Marine—what did he have to say in his letters, and when did she think he might be furloughed? They spoke in mortuary whispers. I'd visited ours in town during that period to view my father's colleagues and friends who'd been killed in combat. More and more, folks spoke in hushed voices about spotting a chaplain knocking on yet another neighbor's door.

Our visits to Beatrice Grange's house often occurred in the late afternoon when the sun's yolk would glaze Chester's pastel cheeks and glance off the silver harps. I badly wanted to lift one to my lips and accompany the women's sad conversations, for I sensed that one day we'd climb the porch stairs of Chester's bungalow and the blue star would have turned to gold.

In fact, when we'd sit in the airless living room on overstuffed furniture decorated with crocheted antimacassars, I imagined Chester had already come home. Not in his Marine blues, mind you. But his ghost. For when the women leaned close to each other, shaking their heads, often grievously, about the murderous Krauts and all the terrible things that were occurring in the Pacific, I imagined Chester was holding off until he could find the courage to say—"I'm dead."

"You sure Chester is still alive, Ma?" I inquired the day she drove the back roads home.

"Why do you ask?"

"'Cause it feels like we're visiting the undertaker's when we go there. The harmonicas clutching his breath—plus that painting of him in his uniform holding rosary beads."

"Chester's still writing to his mother, Jimmy. How could he be deceased?"

But soon the letters stopped. It was as if Mrs. Grange had expected as much, for she quit waiting for the postman. Once, we heard his footsteps on her porch. "Oh, Beatrice," Mother exclaimed, "maybe they'll be some word from Chester."

Her friend smiled transcendently and shook her head. "No," she said. "It's only the telephone and electric bills."

I'd seen that beatific expression on a mural over the alter in church when Jesus announced He was going to visit his Father.

Any day I thought the gold star would hang in Chester's window and one of the harmonicas from his shrine would surely be mine.

One very sultry afternoon that May, Mother and I sat in the now shade-drawn living room quietly observing Mrs. Grange with all the silver instruments in her lap. She took a hankie with brocaded irises and, as if she were cleaning eyeglasses, brought each harp to her lips, exhaled hot air, and briskly polished its silver bright, catching her grimace in a few.

Not one word passed between Ma and her until she lifted the giant chromatic one with a plunger on its side. She studied it intently before bringing it to her nose, closed her eyes, and inhaled deeply. Her face grew radiant.

"Rose," she whispered. "It's Chester, isn't it? Go ahead. Tell me that isn't my boy who'd awaken me in the middle of the night, naked as a blue jay, trembling. 'What is it, Chester?' I'd ask. 'What's wrong?' He'd reply, 'I don't want the Gestapo to take you away, Mama.' I'd laugh, Rose. But the dear shivered like he'd caught a chill. Then I said, 'You're afraid of dying, aren't you, Son?' That's when he wept."

She handed the harmonica to my mother who took a deep whiff of the air holes—lingered—then handed it back.

"What's it smell like to you, Rose?"

"Tree bark," Mother said.

Mrs. Grange nodded as if she had been told the God's truth. She promptly bundled all the harmonicas into the center of her dress, lifted its hem to form a basket, waddled over to the mantle, and returned them to their rightful place—except one.

The chromatic one, long as a schoolhouse ruler, she handed to me. "Blow in it, Jimmy. Chester's dead."

Mother was glum on our trip home. I immediately went up to my room, closed the door, and began running my mouth over the magnificent harp. To me it sounded like an *orkestra*.

That afternoon and into the darkness I blew and drew air across its reeds, making the most wonderful music in progressive tempos—*adagio, allegretto, vivace, accelerando, presto*. My *glissando* solo was most striking of all.

I imagined I came to Chester's instrument with a virtuosity miraculously achieved, that the *Semper Fi's* mastery of the instrument had been providentially passed to me. As if his breath was, indeed, inside the reeds and, since he could no longer expand his lungs, I was doing it for him. Within a week, Mother would take me to Beatrice Grange's house where there would be a gold star in the window and I'd regale her with a concert in her fallen son's honor.

Each Friday in Mrs. Gresham's music class at Rose Avenue Elementary, our fifth grade was serenaded by her rhythm band. Its members kept rotating depending on whom she handed the various tambourines, sand blocks, castanets, triangles, and rhythm sticks out of the coffin-like chest alongside her upright piano.

That week I took my Hohner Chrominica to school.

"A Marine who's fighting the Krauts gave me his prize harmonica, Mrs. Gresham.

I'd like to perform for the class."

She shot me a dubious glance. "You know how to play the harmonica?"

"Yes ma'am, I do. Lieutenant Chester Grange, OSS, taught me how."

I held it to my mouth and pressed the silver plunger several times to give her the impression that I knew exactly what I was doing.

"Are you sure, Jimmy?"

"Scouts honor," I replied.

The rhythm band had already assembled before the blackboard.

"Jimmy Rogues is going to serenade us today, class," she announced.

I stood before my friend Jack Murphy who played the sand blocks.

When I exhibited the prodigious instrument, several classmates stared at me incredulously. A few tittered.

"What tune are you going to play for us, Jimmy?" Mrs. Gresham asked.

"Night Rain," I said. "It's my very own composition."

I'd been blowing and drawing on the air holes all week long, and I would demonstrate the entire range of the harp's *orkestra* effects. One I'd really worked on was sliding it back and forth between my lips like I was wetting a jumbo cigarette paper, but rapidly, while pumping the octave plunger mercilessly.

It would lift them out of their seats.

I started out *adagio*, creating a long, low train whistle. They could appreciate that. Then as the locomotive gained on us—*allegretto, allegro*—I began jumping octaves.

Soon, I was so into blowing and sucking all the wind I could muster that the classmates began snorting. Mrs. Gresham cracked her heels against the hardwood floor in an effort to shush them. Jack Murphy had begun playing the sand blocks behind his head; the castanet duo mocked Lone Ranger and Tonto's horses slowing to a trot; Betsy Tinsley struck the silver "attention, class" bell on Mrs. Gresham's desk with her triangle mallet; and the tambourine trio feigned gagging while whacking the instruments on the heads of the rhythm stick Calucca twins.

By now, I was wheezing and sucking *prestissimo* and my face had turned beet-red as I approached the apogee of "Night Rain"—when Mrs. Gresham peremptorily yanked the chromatic out of my mouth and snapped that I sit down.

The band dropped their instruments into the large chest and quickly slid into their seats.

I began to cry.

"Well," she spat, "you said you knew how to play the . . . MOUTH ORGAN."

"I do," I said.

"What was that we just heard?"

My classmates clasped their hands over their mouths.

"A symphony for Chester Grange—*a dead Marine*."

"Oh." She took a deep breath, a blush creeping up her neck. "Yes—well, give James a nice hand, class." While the students politely applauded, Murphy put his fingers to his lips and made an earsplitting whistle.

"But wait," I said, "I'm not finished."

Before she could object I began playing *Taps*. That I'd truly mastered in my bedroom over the days. I'd made it sound like a coronet. All single notes and just as mournful. It was really Chester's breath, not mine. He was playing at his own graveside, breathing his own requiem.

Now the classmates sat soberly, all wide-eyed and beginning to look forlorn, for most had a brother, father, uncle, or close family friend who had perished in the war. It had touched every street in our town it seemed. Gold stars on white flags were multiplying outside drawn Venetian blinds or opaque green shades.

Once, poster cards hung in some of the windows, informing the iceman how much to drop off that day—a 25 pound or 50 pound block. Now, stars of the dead.

And the mute basketball court behind our school where many of the young warriors once congregated at dusk had swallowed their raucous laughter. But in this moment I imagined the dead souls rising out of the cracked macadam with Marine Band harps to begin singing final breaths they'd rationed for their loved ones—and the skirts who appeared after dark to burnish the nickel plated night its chill—echoing Chester's requiem.

The haunting cry of *Taps* reverberated down the school building's terrazzo hallways. I could hear classroom doors opening for now Chester was bitterly inspired, and he played a second chorus even more plaintive than the first.

I watched Mrs. Gresham sink into her desk chair and drop her head into her hands. The children laid their heads onto their desks, too, and some began to weep.

And I felt ashamed holding Chester's harmonica while he was performing. I felt like a paper soldier, for I'd done nothing except smell his breath.

And pretend I was a musician.

While he was the star.

The Author Speaks!

I wrote this piece during the most intense period of the recent war in Iraq. Feeling distressed over the loss of our soldiers and the citizens of Iraq, I recalled that, as a boy during World War II, the gold star banners began multiplying in the living room windows of the houses on my street, and it made me sad and confused.

Questions:

1. How would you describe the connection in Jimmy's mind between his awareness of Chester's death and his desire to own the dead soldier's harmonica? Was he more fascinated with playing and performing on the instrument than he was saddened by Chester's death?

2. What are the signs in Beatrice Grange's house that led Jimmy to believe that her son was no longer alive?

3. What effect do the rhythm band's antics have, if any, on the story?

4. Does Jimmy's playing Taps effect the outcome of the story? If so, how?

Julie Shigekuni

Elephant Story

Within weeks of entering the fifth grade Nora had become hopelessly enchanted by Mr. Weissgarten, whose ideas and classroom practices were quite different from what she'd been taught at Sunday School. Mr. Weissgarten read stories to the class every day after lunch and reserved the first half hour of each morning for the students to write random thoughts in their notebooks. Nora spent her days making up stories that might please her teacher, but her favorite activity came in the early afternoons when Mr. Weissgarten would shut off the fluorescent overhead lighting in favor of the shadows that filled the room with mystery. She liked the dark, curly hair that he wore long, pulled back in a tight ponytail so that his wire-rimmed glasses accentuated the sharp angles of his face. In the darkness, while he stared down at the pages of a book, she memorized his face.

One afternoon he began a story about a young girl named Yoshiko whose family was forced by the American government to evacuate its home. She had heard the word *evacuate* only in the context of emergencies: bomb threats, fire drills, earthquakes. She did not understand the story fully but sat spellbound and self-conscious, too, of the mix of fascination and horror that it stirred in her. Yoshiko being a Japanese-American girl, she felt somehow implicated. Then, that same afternoon, Mr. Weissgarten pulled Nora aside after class to ask if her parents had been interned in relocation camps during the Second World War. She had no idea whether they had or hadn't, but, since it did not seem appropriate to answer in the negative, she nodded blankly, hoping that her oblique response would satisfy her beloved teacher.

To her dismay, she was instead given the task of interviewing her parents and then of spending the week recording her thoughts in her notebook. While Mr. Weissgarten informed her that this assignment was optional, offered as a suggestion that she should undertake only insofar as she wished, she was no stranger to unspoken commands, and she took on her assignment as solemnly as she would a severe punishment.

For reasons she could not identify, her response to Mr. Weissgarten's suggestion caused an ache in the pit of her stomach that when she got home she described to her mother as sickness. Believing her daughter completely, Yukari felt Nora's forehead, then sent her to her room. And perhaps she really had become ill, because, when Yukari came to inquire as to whether Nora was well enough to help with dinner, she found Nora asleep.

Nora would have stayed that way, letting the evening pass into morning, except that it was her job to help with dinner, and so she roused herself from bed. Seated on the stool where she worked across the counter from her mother she could feel the sickness return. She could not formulate her question into words and instead watched Yukari, her expertise evident in each pop as her hands worked the ends off a pile of long beans. A fly buzzed overhead, annoying her as she swept the stray hairs from her face with her wrist. When the long beans were ready to be cooked, she carried them away to a pot of water that boiled on the stove. Then, returning to the counter where Nora sat, Yukari clapped her hands together over her head, plucking the fly from mid-air and startling Nora out of her thoughts.

"What did you learn in school today?" Yukari asked, as was her habit.

"Nothing," Nora shrugged, the question she needed to ask still refusing to gather words in her head.

"Then you should pay better attention." Her mother dismissed her, returning to the stove where steam rose from pots of various sizes.

"Mr. Weissgarten told us a story about a girl whose family was *evacuated*," she said at last.

"Ah," Yukari smiled. "You're learning about history."

"Yes." Nora returned her mother's smile cautiously. "Mr. Weissgarten said I should interview you and Dad about the relocation camps."

"Let me tell you what I know about history," Yukari began unexpectedly, and, enthused that the conversation that she had so dreaded seemed to be going well, Nora awaited the thing that her mother, who did not ordinarily tell stories, might say.

"Where I grew up in Hiroshima, there was a zoo," she said, and then she stopped.

Nora sat up straight and perched on the edge of her chair to show her attentiveness. Yukari eyed her before launching into her story. "The zoo was famous in the area because back then there weren't very many zoos around. But during the war, the military were ordered to kill the animals. There was no one left to take care of them and what food there was could not be spared. So one by one the innocent animals were slaughtered until, finally, the only ones left were the elephants.

"The elephants, as you might guess, had been the most popular attraction, beloved by everyone who visited them. They were also massive animals, and even men who had been specially trained as soldiers did not know how to kill one. So, as it happened after protest by the townspeople, the military decided to let them live. They didn't have the heart, so, in the end, guess what happened?"

"What?" Nora asked, bemused.

"In the end, the elephants wound up starving to death."

Nora did not know how to respond to this strange story her mother told, but perhaps she had not been listening. Intent on getting what she needed for her notebook, she was concerned only that the information she sought did not appear to be forthcoming. "I thought you were going to tell me about getting evacuated," she said at last.

"I *am* telling you," Yukari retorted. "I'm telling you that it was wartime, and that horrible things were happening everywhere."

She had nothing more to say. Earlier that semester, Mr. Weissgarten had mentioned the word *ambivalence*. He said it was about two opposite and strong feelings existing side by side, and, though she had forgotten the definition, the word popped into her head as she sat and watched her mother put the final touches on their dinner.

The Author Speaks!

I'm interested in the things people don't say when they're talking to each other; I think what isn't said sometimes gives as much information as what is said. I grew up with a mother who expected me to learn by watching. Likewise, the dramatic action in this story comes from Nora's mother's indirect explanation. While a failure to communicate guides the exchange between Nora and her mother, I hope you'll also find some other, important things going on here between the characters.

Questions:

1. Discuss what you knew about internment prior to reading this story. In what ways is internment the subject of this story? What else is this story about?

2. Why do you think Nora was hesitant to ask her mother about internment?

3. It could be said that Nora's mother offers the elephant story to justify internment. What is your response to the analogy Yukari draws? Why else do you suppose Yukari might have chosen this occasion to tell the elephant story?

4. What clues do you have about when this story takes place? How important is the time period to this piece?

5. Project Nora's relationship with her mother into the future and write a conversation recalling the elephant story that might take place between them twenty years from the time of this scene.

6. Compare Nora's relationship to her mother to another relationship in literature or in your life.

Greg Sanders

Demise of the Buffalo, Circa 1880

Unable to sleep, Kyle turned on his bedside lamp and sat up. He noticed something very small on the sheet by his arm. At first he thought it was simply a piece of dust or lint. Everything in his room had a place and although he was half-asleep, he knew that this spot did not belong on his sheet by his arm. Then it moved, just barely, and his first instinct was to flatten it. But he hesitated, because it moved so almost imperceptibly, didn't hop or fly away as he'd expect an insect would. No, there was something about this creature—if it was a creature—that made Kyle reconsider.

He squinted and stared as best he could, close up. A flea? No, not black and shiny, and anyway fleas made him itch as soon as he saw one, and he wasn't itching. His cats got fleas almost every summer, and this was the middle of the winter, so fleas were out. Again he stared but saw only something alive yet unidentifiable. Closer. Maybe it was a beetle, some miniscule South American species that had gotten lost, or maybe a gnat or even a mite. He'd never seen a mite, but this could be his introduction to one. He reached for his magnifying glass, which he kept in a drawer in his bedside table. He moved the bedside lamp closer to shed more light on the subject at hand. Because this thing was on his bright, bleached-white sheets, it was well contrasted and through the magnifying glass it was very large, defined perfectly, and undeniably a buffalo.

It kicked a little, as if dust would fly in its wake, and wagged its tail with what could only be described as impatience, as if it would rather not be on Kyle's sheets. It shook its shaggy mane. Never had Kyle seen a buffalo that would fit under his fingernail. But certainly that's what it was, and it turned its head and looked out from its hilly cotton terrain at Kyle, and he could see its eyes, and he decided that the buffalo was lost. After considering again what to do, he realized he was tired and had a long day ahead tomorrow, so he crushed the buffalo between his fingers. It left a tiny wet spot and he went to wash his hands and have a glass of water. Then he turned the lights off and fell back asleep.

In the morning when he told his parents there had been a very small buffalo on his sheets, they didn't believe him. When he told his friends at school about the buffalo they laughed at him and thought he was crazy. He could tell they thought he was joshing them. Finally, he told his science teacher that he'd seen a tiny buffalo on his sheets.

"Well what did you do with it then?" she said.

"I killed it," Kyle said.

"Oh, that's a shame. Don't you think we'd like to see a tiny buffalo too? Why did you kill it?"

"I was tired," Kyle replied.

"Well that might have been the last little buffalo on the planet."

That night he stayed up late looking at his sheets, examining the smallest of spots, but he never saw a tiny buffalo again.

The Author Speaks!

Here is a rather strange story, the first draft of which I wrote many years ago. I wasn't quite sure where it came from, other than some playful, and dark, part of my imagination. I think all of us have awakened in the middle of the night and found a tiny bug somewhere close by—a mosquito, a ladybug, an ant. But Kyle found something entirely different. Would you do what Kyle did? My answer is a decisive *no*.

Ron Koertge

Just a Couple of Girls Talking Haiku

I walk my dad to work because then it's like I'm taking care of him for a change instead of the other way around all the time.

Not that he needs taking care of especially. Where we live, there are always people sitting out on their steps or maybe just in a second story window. If anybody tried to steal my dad's money or give him a hard time, somebody would yell or dial 911. Or both.

Most people would. Not all, I guess. Dad works in a Community Development office about two blocks from our apartment. Basically he decides if a street gets some money or a park, if Mr. Jamal gets a no-interest loan instead of Mr. Nguyen. So not everybody likes him all the time.

That's probably why I jump when some punk kid from all the way across the street sees a white guy in a Lexus, throws something at him, and yells, "Get outta here, honkey."

Dad pulls me a little closer. "Honkey is a really interesting word."

"I'm not afraid. I know that kid. He's okay."

"Do you want to know the honkey-story for your word book or not?"

"Sure. It'll give me something to tell my children when we're all gathered around the fire and the wind is howling outside."

"You read too much."

I pull at his beard, which is so blonde and so short it's almost not a beard at all. "And the story is. . . ?"

"Oh, yeah. Well, the story is that white guys used to park outside a theatre in Harlem and when the black actresses came out, they'd honk at them. So pretty soon all white people are honkeys."

"Why did they honk at them?"

He gives me that look, the one that says we-talked-about-this-so-don't-act dumb. I say, "Oh."

Dad glances down the street. The boy who yelled at the Lexus is showing off for his friends. "When did Oscar shave his head?"

"Maybe a week ago."

He squats down, puts his lunch bag on the sidewalk. "I'll walk you to school if you want, keep the local Oscars off your case."

"Oh, yeah. That's a really good idea. " I have a pretty much bottomless supply of scorn when I need it.

"Then I'll see you tonight. I talked to Mrs. Werlin. She'll be right there when you get back from school. Like always."

"Mrs. Werlin smells."

"I know."

"She's malodorous."

"She's fulsome."

That stops me until I come up with, "Putrid!"

He thinks hard, then gives up. Or pretends to. He could probably beat me in Battle of the Adjectives if he wanted to. He was a poet once. But he gave that up when he and Mom split. Then he lost his hotshot dot-com job. And we moved from the burbs. The two of us.

I walk him right to his office and wave to Rachel who sits at a desk by the window. Before I kiss him good-bye, I say, "I'm taking the long way to school, okay? Past the old Bradley Building. That mural's supposed to be done and Mrs. Paz says we have to take a good look at it because there's going to be some kind of assignment."

Dad leans down. "Okay. But no further than the Bradley Building, and try and find somebody to walk with."

That turns out to be easy, because there are lots of people headed that way. More and more all the time, like folks coming out of their houses after a bad storm.

A bunch of us round the corner at Webster and Seventy-second, and there it is! Even the traffic slows down to look at the colossal, mammoth, voluminous mural of a girl sitting on the ground in the back yard of a building just like the one I live in. There's a wire fence and, further off, the wooden one. Laundry hanging from two tall poles. A fire escape, and, beyond that, a smidgen of sky. She has her back to everybody, and I like her a lot.

A little boy right beside me looks up at his mom. "What's it for?"

She scowls. "Whatever it's for, the money could have been better spent."

Mr. Bauer says it's going to turn out be nothing but a big ad for something nobody needs, anyway. Mr. Solis claims that when the crowd gets big enough, the INS is going to show up and check green cards.

I wonder why it has to be for anything? Most of the paintings I've seen on field trips or with Dad aren't for anything; they're just pretty or at least interesting.

But they're always kind of little and from way back in time, too: all those Virgin Marys, for instance. And guys on horses or standing by a big dog. But this mural is vast! And it's about where I live. That girl up there could be me.

At school, I walk in my English class to see a three-line poem on the board.

First full moon this year. (5)

Poor thing! Look how it's tangled (7)

in that spindly tree. (5)

I have to admit it's cool to feel sorry for the moon! And I like how when I close my eyes I can see the picture in the poem just as clear as I can see our mural.

Mrs. Paz talks about how old some haiku are, how they're almost always just seventeen syllables long, how they don't rhyme.

She writes a few more on the board. There are lots of lotus blossoms and frogs.

Then Mrs. Paz says, "Now write a haiku about the new mural in our neighborhood."

Everybody moans like she said there's going to be snake-on-a-stick for lunch. Mrs. Paz just looks out the window and nibbles a carrot stick.

For awhile, I think I'm not going to finish. I start a couple of times, but don't get anyplace. The first one has a frog in it, but there isn't a frog in the mural, so that's dumb. Then I start to think about my mother. All of a sudden words pretty much come up from inside the paper and meet my pen. I don't even count the syllables.

Get up off the ground,

Maureen. Do something useful.

Go wash the dishes.

That's the way my mother talked. A lot of the time. Oh, man. I have to swallow hard. I have to bite my lip. I can see the headlines now LOCAL HONKEY CRIES OVER POEM. No way.

I try again. It's harder this time. I scratch my head, I count on my fingers. I wad up one piece of paper after another.

When Mrs. Paz collects everyone's poem, I show her my pathetic rough drafts and shrug. She says not to worry and walks to the board. She takes her time sifting through the pages in her hand. Then she picks up some chalk and writes:

The clothes of a girl

who drowned in the clouds can look

like someone's washing.

Mrs. Paz points to the second line. "This is particularly lovely. Look how the sounds in *drowned* and *clouds* cuddle up to each other. And the whole thing is very mysterious. Good work, Lola."

What? Everybody turns around. Nobody knows anything about Lola Vargas except her name. She's got such a bad stutter she never says a word. Not in class. Not out of class. She drifts in and out of the room like a real ghost. A ghost who stutters. B,b,b,b,b boo.

Amazing.

When class is over, two or three kids bump Lola on purpose. A big girl named Rosie Olivares, says, "G,g, guh, guh good w,w,wuh, wuh work, luh, luh luh, Lola." And everybody laughs.

I swing my backpack around, reach in, whip out my notebook with a flourish, and write as big as I can

WHEN A BIRD SINGS THE
SAME NOTE OVER AND OVER
SHE'S NOT STUTTERING

That shuts them up. And I'm as knocked out as they are. First of all, where did that come from? Second of all, nobody stands up to Rosie Olivares, who's got a homemade tattoo you can see and a couple more that everybody says only Hector gets to look at. There are boys, lots of boys, who are afraid of Rosie because the word is she carries a razor blade in her hair.

Rosie stares down at my notebook. Nobody says one word. Lola moves a little closer to me.

Finally Rosie gives a little snort. "Who cares about a couple of losers." Then she swaggers away.

Mrs. Paz steps out into the hall. "Is there trouble?"

"No, ma'am."

"Then I'd go to my next class."

Lola nods. I say, "Yes, ma'am."

Next morning on the way to school, Lola appears. She doesn't say anything. She still trudges like always. But I'm usually on my own, too, so it's kind of cool to walk with somebody.

When we pass the mural, I give her a little nudge and point. She nods and even smiles.

I start thinking that maybe that girl up there isn't me. Maybe it's Lola thinking about what it's like to every day walk into a cage of hostile consonants. I picture her in lace-up boots, khaki pants and one of those African safari hats. She's got a whip and a chair. The k's and d's and b's growl at her.

Then I feel Lola's hand on mine, tugging at me, making me stop. We're closer to school than I thought. There's Rosie's staring at the bike rack. Her jaw is tight and quivery. Her fists are clenched.

We all creep past her, and we barely make it before she goes ballistic: kicking one of the bikes until it goes down, its handlebars like antlers, its body twisted.

"What are you looking at?" shouts Rosie, and everybody scatters. We flee.

In math, I pretend to listen to my teacher, but I'm really thinking that maybe the girl on the mural isn't me or Lola but Rosie taking a minute off from being tough and wishing she lived someplace with a lot more sky.

Which makes me want to write something.

"Did you put this in my locker?" Rosie waves a piece of paper under my nose. We're in the girl's bathroom, and the usual hubbub—the whoosh of the flushing toilets, the roar of girls brushing their hair—disappears.

I nod.

Rosie takes me by the shoulder just like a teacher. "C'mere."

Like I've got a choice.

Out in the hall she points to my poem, the one I wrote in math:

That jacket you bought
him, strapped to the back of her
new, red bicycle.

"How'd you know what Hector did?"

"I saw you kick Latasha's bicycle."

"But how'd you know everything? How'd you know the whole story?"

"You were really mad. I just put two and two together."

"If you're makin' fun of me, I swear to God—"

"I'm not. I'm not making fun of you. I've been that mad."

"You haven't got a boyfriend."

I hesitate, then decide to tell her. "You know how Hector went with another girl and left his new jacket? My mom went with another guy. She came and got her stuff. Almost the only thing she left was this sweater I bought her."

Rosie swallows.

I shrug. "So I know what it's like."

"I'm gonna kick Hector's butt. If you want, I'll get some guys and we'll take care of your mother's hook-up, too."

"She, you know, moved."

"I could find her."

"No, it's okay. Thanks, though."

I lean against the wall. I start to breath again.

After school Lola is waiting for me outside. When she sees me she holds up a piece of paper, kind of like those guys at the airport with a limo outside.

> I'm glad you're okay.
> Rosie would be sorry if
> she ever hurt you.

"Oh, really?"

Lola frowns. She shows me an empty page, then draws three lines. She wants me to speak haiku. So I try.

> What could you do
> to Rosie? You weigh about
> as much as moonlight.

Lola grins. And writes

> Don't worry. I'd just
> get my brothers to break her
> big, fat, ugly legs.

"I didn't know you had brothers."

Lola holds up two fingers. I scribble.

It's just my dad and
me. Which is okay. We get
along pretty well.

Just then, Hector comes out with Latasha. Lola and I look at each other and roll our
eyes. Lola writes,

Have you ever had
a boyfriend? My dad says I'm
too young for that stuff.

"Can I just talk, Lola? You're a lot faster at writing haiku than I am."
    When she nods, I say, "Dad says I'm too young, too. I can't go out until I'm in
high school."

Do you like any
body special? I'll bet they
like your pretty hair.

"Boys are a pain in the butt. I've got better stuff to do than fool around with boys." I
show her my word book. She reads the latest entry, which is the honkey-story my dad
told me. Lola turns the pages, her eyes get ardent.

This is a treasure
chest. It's a gold mine. It's a

She gets stuck. Her tongue comes out. She gets all squinty. I help her out.
    "Repository?"
    She likes that, especially because it's a five-syllable line all by itself.
    I say, "If you want, keep the book. Give it to me tomorrow."

For a little while, Lola is kind of famous. People want to talk to her because she answers with a haiku. Every time. Most kids are nice; they ask her something, wait while she writes, look at it, count the syllables and say "Thank you." Sometimes they want her to sign the poem and give it to them.

There's always a few jerks. Alejondro asks, "What's it like to be a loser?"

> Animals fight and
> get killed. But the fish is smart.
> She sinks to succeed.

That totally shuts him up. Lola just grins and adds it to her collection of Keepers, this peechee folder Mrs. Paz gave her so she could collect the poems she likes the best.

After awhile people forget about her. She was kind of a novelty. Somebody brings a gun to school, and that's the new headline. Somebody else gets a scholarship to a performing arts high school in the city.

By then, though, Lola and I are tight. She comes over to my house after school. We study or watch TV. I let her use my computer. We take turns at the keyboard so we can talk about stuff faster. Mostly we talk about Rosie, how we've been leaving a new haiku in her locker every day. She's gotta like it, because now she smiles at us. Sometimes.

Lola just loves to write poetry. Sometimes we sit at the table after dinner and talk a little haiku. We follow the rules. Everything we say has to be seventeen syllables. We write on scraps of paper and pass them back and forth.

A lot of times these turn out really goofy

> Freaky hairstyles make
> my salt shaker a nervous
> wreck. Pass the pizza.

But the other night we're talking haiku and we come up with this real beauty. Shakespeare doesn't have anything to worry about. But it's still very, very cool. I read it out loud. Lola puts it on the table and feels the lines, like they're Braille or something.

Dad looks over her shoulder. "Can I have this one?" Then he drifts away.

Lola and I start to do the dishs. She likes to wash, I don't mind drying. I turn on the radio and kind of dance. Lola flicks suds at me. I snap the towel at her, then run toward the other room.

Dad glances up at me, then down again. He has a black sketch book on his lap, the kind he used to use.

Oh, my God. He's writing again for the first time since Mom left. He's got our haiku in his left hand:

Words in a line on
a page: little ships on an
amazing white sea.

The Author Speaks!

1. People like to talk about what inspires them to do things. It doesn't have to be about fiction or poetry. Seeing Kobe Bryant play can be inspiring, and not just to play basketball, either, but to do something extraordinary. Some people like (or learn to like) word derivations, so looking up inspiration and talking about all its meanings can be fun; for example, one way the word is used simply means breathing. Does the idea of breathing in an idea get you charged up? Do you think there's such a thing as bad inspiration? Inspiration is usually a pretty lofty word, but can people get inspired to do something bad?

2. What is your experience with poetry? Do you ever read poetry to yourself out loud at home? Do you think there's poetry all around you? A sermon can be poetic, for example; some advertisements are poetic, and there's a famous story about a teacher who told his students he'd seen a poem on his way to school while he was waiting at a corner: WALK WITH LIGHT. Consider the name of an old John Ciardi book—HOW DOES A POEM MEAN? Most poets hate it when people ask, "What does this poem mean?"

3. Try an exercise called "Write Your Novel on a Postcard." Take 20–25 words to sum up your story. Some writers do this all the time so they have the essential story in their heads before they start to write sentence-by-sentence, chapter-by-chapter.

   Remember two Ps: What's the problem? (What dilemma is your character facing that has to be resolved?) What's the plan? (What's your main character doing to solve the problem?) If you get stuck, think of something simple and direct: Bob has to get his sister to the doctor, and there's a big storm. Flesh out the rest.

4. See if you can think of a story where nobody and nothing changes very much. Consider the basic conflicts in narrative: man vs. man, man vs. nature, man vs. himself. In the first one, something as simple as a fight can cause someone to change. She resolves to not do that again or he resolves to train harder next time. Do you think it's possible to resolve any of those basic conflicts and have nothing change?

5. Usually, really good stories are like finely tuned machines that don't run as well when they're tinkered with or changed. Try changing things in this story. For example, could the narrator have been a boy, and would the story be the same? Would it matter if the narrator lived with her mom instead of her dad? What if Lola or Rosie had been Larry or Robert?

Douglas Thorpe

All Things Counter, Original, Spare, Strange . . .

It's a Thursday afternoon in March as I sit at the B&O Espresso Café in Seattle and ponder upon things. The Beatles play in the background.

Tell my why you cried
And why you lied to me

I glance outside and see a young woman standing at the corner waiting for the flow of traffic to break. The wind blows back her hair; one hand is in the pocket of her jeans as she twirls her keys with the other. She watches the cars go by, her eyes following the curve of the road down a hill created millennia ago by glaciers, a hill recently walked by the Duwamish on their way to what we now call Puget Sound.

The song plays on. Clouds move slowly across the sky.

Randomly I open a book and read about balance, how most of us achieve it only through effort: our balance, the writer says, is really "a resistance to falling over." But this is not balance. This is ". . . a state of contraction, of holding things together so they will not fall apart."

We think of justice as balance, Heller writes, as in a set of scales "poised and standing still between two extremes." But this too gives a false image: "In reality, equally weighted and balanced scales sway constantly, gently, and gracefully about their middle point." Balance is found in motion, as we understand when we learn to ride a bike. "Balance is not a static condition, but a process of constant flux, a fluid expression of wholeness and ease."

I imagine a tennis player poised to return a serve, rocking gently from side to side exactly as I've seen chi gung masters rock, breathing softly between movements. I think as well of guitar players on stage, eyes closed as they listen to the band around them, as they attend to the bass player, the drummer, the keyboards, the singer and even the audience. They rock to the music, attending to some rhythm so deep that we really don't have words for it. It's something ordered and yet *constantly emerging*.

Is this chaos or creation?

In a well-known Taoist story, "Shu (Brief) and Hu (Sudden) go to visit Hun-dun (Chaos), who graciously offers them his hospitality. Observing that Hun-dun lacks the seven openings through which men see, hear, eat and breathe, Shu and Hu determine to create them. Each day they bore a new hole. On the seventh day, Hun-dun dies."

Although surely unintentional, it's a beautiful inversion of the Biblical creation story, where on the seventh day God rests from his labors of dividing light from dark and in this way imposing order on chaos. Not surprisingly, in the west this "defeat" of Hun-dun has frequently been understood as a triumph of good over evil.

In Chuang Tzu, however, the story has a far different moral.

Hun-dun has no openings; he cannot be penetrated. Shu and Hu see this as a problem in Hun-dun, whom they cannot understand. How, after all, do you make sense of that which has no senses when it's through the senses that we learn to make sense? But Hun-dun is not to be grasped. As one writer says, he "is not so much a word but a way, or ways, of viewing the world."

Scholars suggest that the word Hun-dun resembles the words *tao* and *wu*—usually translated as "nothingness." But rather than being void of substance and without creative potential, this emptiness contains everything. This chaos *is* potential, a word with its roots in the word *potent*, as in powerful. "Chaos" is implicit in creation just as all creativity involves chaos—as any artist or scientist knows.

We find this same relationship between chaos and creation everywhere in nature and in art. Consider the idea of syncopation: it's a brief break in rhythm, a weak beat between two strong beats creating a new rhythm through its relationship to the order surrounding it.

"We are here because of the broken symmetries," science writer George Johnson similarly suggests:

The theorists tell us that in the early moments of a perfectly crystalline creation there would have been an equal amount of matter and antimatter. But it seems that a random fluctuation, a broken symmetry, led to matter's having the slightest edge—a billion and one quarks for every billion antiquarks, perhaps. After most of these particles and antiparticles killed each other off, there was just enough matter left to make a universe.

"In a perfect, undifferentiated world," Johnson concludes, "we wouldn't exist."

Balance, I'm thinking: it's *Hun-dun*.

I put down my pen and sit just for a moment inside this stillness, this sense I suddenly have of arriving at some kind of strange and hilarious glory. It's really nothing; at the next table two friends share a joke, laughing aloud, their forks briefly poised in the air. I hear the sound of the espresso machine and look outside in time to see the woman cross the street, climb into her truck, and pull into the flow of traffic.

Well I gave you everything I had
Tell me what and I'll apologize

It's all clouds and coffee, all curve and rhythm. It's a billion random choices which somehow taken together end up looking like a dance. The word "chaos" doesn't even begin to name it. Call it mercy, *chesed,* the love that moves the sun and the other stars. Call it the *Tao*—even then it will take the sublime poetry of the *Taoteching* to give us a glimpse of what this way really is—of its power and grace, and of its delight, as the poet Gerard Manley Hopkins said, in "all things counter, original, spare, strange . . ."

Praise her.

The Author Speaks!

Questions:

1. Where in your own life do you experience something of this idea of balance? In sports? In music? In mathematics or poetry or song?

2. Is there a relationship between literal balance (riding a bike, balancing on one leg) and balance as a more general idea? What does it mean to live a "balanced life"? To eat a "balanced diet"?

3. Explore the Chinese concept of yin/yang. How does it relate to this idea of a balance between chaos and order?

4. Draw Hun-dun.

5. Read the story of creation in *The Book of Genesis*. Read a Native American story of creation. Compare them.

6. Write your own creation story.

STEVEN SCHUTZMAN

Chelm Goes To War

Synopsis: In order to end Chelm's poverty, the city council votes to make war on Gorshkov, an equally small and poor village. Things go hilariously wrong when switched road signs lead the frying pan-wielding Chelmite warriors back to Chelm and they believe they have entered a mirror world.

Characters:
SHLEMIEL
GRONAM OX
DOPEY LEKISH
ZEINVEL NINNY
SENDER DONKEY
SHMENDRICK NUMSKULL
TREITEL FOOL
CHELMITE ONE
CHELMITE TWO
CHELMITE THREE
RABBI
SENDER'S WIFE
TREITEL'S WIFE
GRONAM'S WIFE

Since all CHELMITES *wear fake beards, they can be played by either male or female actors. Smaller roles can be double or triple cast or more. For example a single actress can play all* THREE WIVES, CHELMITES ONE, TWO, AND THREE, *and the* RABBI. *In addition, except for* SHLEMIEL *and* GRONAM, COUNCIL MEMBERS' *roles may be combined so those five roles become three. With artful casting, the whole cycle can be done with six or seven actors.*

Scene 1

COUNCIL OF CHELM, *Council Members* SHMENDRICK NUMSKULL, ZEINVEL NINNY, SENDER DONKEY, TREITEL FOOL, DOPEY LEKISH, *and* GRONAM OX. *Plus* SHLEMIEL *with pen and parchment.*

SHLEMIEL
(*To* AUDIENCE)
Here ye. Here ye. Attention. Attention. Quiet down everybody. By the decree of our Great Sage and Leader, Gronam Ox, the Council of Chelm is now called into emergency session. But, before the meeting begins, as our tradition dictates, our Great Sage and Leader Gronam Ox will answer the difficult questions brought to him by the ordinary people of Chelm.

GRONAM *stands.* CHELMITES *line up to ask questions.*

CHELMITE ONE
O Great Thinker Gronam, could you tell me please, why does the dog wag his tail?

GRONAM
Because the dog is stronger than the tail. Were it the other way around the tail would wag the dog.

CHELMITE TWO
O Wiseman Gronam, I've been wondering, why is the ocean salty?

GRONAM

You know how salty herring is when you eat it. Well, the ocean is salty from all the herring swimming around in the water.

CHELMITE THREE

O Sage of Sages, I'm puzzled by something: My father had a great beard and yet here I am 40 years old with a few hairs on my cheek, practically beardless. How can this be? What became of the law of heredity?

GRONAM

You are beardless because of the law of heredity. But you don't take after your father, you take after your mother.

SHLEMIEL

(*To* AUDIENCE)

No further proof is needed: Gronam Ox is the wisest man in all of Chelm. But, please, pay me no mind at all. Among these Great Sages, Shlemiel, that's me, is a mere nothing. And that's why they made me Council Secretary, according to Decree 1467:

TREITEL

"It is decreed that Shlemiel, who lacks our wisdom because his mother wasn't born in Chelm, is forbidden to speak at council meetings. He is only allowed to write down what we sages say, for the benefit of future generations."

SHLEMIEL

(*To* AUDIENCE)

So I became the historian of Chelm, known throughout the world as the "village of fools." Now the world may call us fools but as the council decreed in Decree 7897 . . .

ZEINVEL

"It is decreed that we Chelmites are not fools. It's just that foolish things are always happening to us."

SHLEMIEL

(*To* AUDIENCE)

And Decree 7898, I remember very well how that one came about.

SHMENDRICK

"It is decreed to be against the law to use the words 'fools' and 'Chelm' in the same sentence. Anyone found using the word 'fools' and 'Chelm' in the same sentence will have his thoughts changed."

SENDER

But you just did it, Shmendrick. Twice.

SHMENDRICK

Did what?

SENDER

Used 'fools' and 'Chelm' in a sentence. Your law broke the law.

ZEINVEL

It's a no good law that breaks the law.

TREITEL

For if our laws keep breaking each other . . .

DOPEY

. . . then all we'll have is a bunch of broken laws lying around like broken dishes . . .

SENDER

... and then and then won't all our wisdom be like a delicious soup with no bowls for the people to eat it from?

ZEINVEL

And then and then and then if we can't make any more laws how will we get away from our wives for council meetings?

ALL

WOE IS US.

SHLEMIEL

(*To* AUDIENCE)

As you see, our sages ponder their way deeply into every problem.

ALL

WOE IS US. WOE IS US. WOE IS US.

GRONAM

Sages, sages, please calm yourselves. A law can't break the law, for that would be unlawful.

SHLEMIEL

Forgive me, Gronam, but doesn't God's law say "Thou shalt not kill"?

GRONAM

And your point is, Shlemiel?

SHLEMIEL

The gallows at the center of town, O Great Rabbi.

ZEINVEL

But we're not killing anybody, Shlemiel, we're executing them.

GRONAM

Thank you, Zeinvel. Now please, Shlemiel, don't speak anymore.
Just write.

SHLEMIEL

(*To* AUDIENCE)
So I recorded what happened that day and every day after, always
writing my fingers off. But today Chelm faces terrible trouble and
that's why Gronam Ox has called the sages to emergency session.

GRONAM

Chelm is in crisis. Our citizens don't have enough to eat, they dress
in rags and suffer from colds making them unable to work. How
can we solve this crisis? Think, my Sages, think with all your might
for seven days and seven nights.

SHLEMIEL

(*To* AUDIENCE *as* COUNCIL *pantomimes what he says*)
And so as day follows night and night follows day our Sages thought
and thought. They thought standing and sitting in chairs. They
thought up one side and down the other. They thought by pulling
their beards, wrinkling their foreheads, and pacing the floor.

GRONAM

Time's up. Let's hear what you have to say. Sender Donkey.

SENDER

There are very few people in Chelm educated enough to know that
'crisis' means a desperate situation. If we make a law forbidding

education, no one will ever know there is a crisis and we won't have to wrack our brains in order to solve it.

GRONAM

Hmmm. Zeinvel Ninny.

ZEINVEL

We should declare two fast days each week, namely Monday and Thursday. It's not that we have too little food, it's that we have too much eating.

GRONAM

Hmmm. What about the scarcity of clothing? Shmendrick Numskull.

SHMENDRICK

I say we put high taxes on clothing. The poor won't be able to afford clothes, and that will leave plenty for the rich. Why worry about the poor?

GRONAM

Hmmm. Dopey Lekish.

DOPEY

At night, when the rich are asleep, the poor should break in and steal their clothes. Then the poor will be properly dressed and able to work in the fields without catching cold. Why worry about the rich?

GRONAM

Hmmm. It seems seven days and seven nights of pondering have not been enough and you must think on it again.

SHLEMIEL

(*To* AUDIENCE)

And so our Council of Sages thought once more. They thought until the left sides of their brains went numb and the right sides of their brains dropped dead. They thought until . . . nevermind.

GRONAM

Time's up. Shmendrick.

SHMENDRICK

We should give all the bread to some people and no bread at all to other people who will then starve to death allowing those who are left to take their clothes. That kills two birds with one stone.

SENDER

Idiot! Do you know how long it takes for folks to starve to death? I ask you: do we want those left to spend all that time freezing their tooshes off?

TREITEL

I know: why not ask the starving to kill themselves immediately, since they're going to die anyway, and avoid all that unnecessary suffering?

SHLEMIEL

May I point out, O Wisemen, that though everyone's going to die sooner or later, they hardly ever appreciate being rushed.

GRONAM

Please, Shlemiel. Don't speak. Just write. My esteemed Sages, though your solutions are good ones, I have come up with the solution of solutions. My solution is so good that, after it solves this problem, there will be plenty of solution left over to solve other problems we still have lying around. My solution is that only a war can save Chelm. We must go to war.

SHLEMIEL

War?!!! You mean with killing, dying, bloodshed, freezing to death in the snow, and other forms of terrible suffering.

ZEINVEL

Please, Shlemiel. A war with whom, Gronam?

GRONAM

A war with the people of Gorshkov.

SHMENDRICK

But what have the people of Gorshkov done that we should make war on them?

SENDER

And we have no weapons. Even Pechele, the town policeman, carries only a stick.

GRONAM

We will make war on Gorshkov because they call us fools. And while it is true we have no weapons, we do have Zalman the Blacksmith to make swords for us by melting the pots and pans our wives cook with.

TREITEL

I don't think my wife will let me have her pots and pans, Gronam.

SHMENDRICK

Mine either. And such a temper my wife's got, I can't tell you.

ZEINVEL

Your wife? What about mine? I'd rather fight Gorshkov any day.

DOPEY

But how can a war with Gorshkov help us? Gorshkov is a small village even poorer than we are.

GRONAM

When we win the war, we will make slaves of our enemies and they will make us rich.

A pause. The SAGES all look at each other.

SENDER

Hooray for Gronam Ox!!!

ALL

HOORAY!!!! HOORAY!!!

TREITEL

Gronam Ox will be King of Chelm and Emperor of Gorshkov.

SHLEMIEL *meekly raises his hand.*

GRONAM

What is it now, Shlemiel?

SHLEMIEL

Super Sage, Future King and Emperor, Gorshkov is far from here, through a big, dark forest, how will our brave soldiers find their way?

Another pause. The SAGES look at each other.

ZEINVEL

Such a malicious question is a betrayal of the empire.

SENDER

Down with Shlemiel!

SHMENDRICK

He should be imprisoned until the end of the world.

DOPEY

Forget prison: He should be hanged.

TREITEL

To hang him once isn't enough: he should be hanged three times.

GRONAM

My Sages, let's not be too hard on Shlemiel who can't help being foolish since his mother wasn't born in Chelm. But still he should be taught a lesson. Therefore we will send Shlemiel as a spy to Gorshkov to scout the best way there.

SHLEMIEL

But, but, I hate war. I'm a peace loving man.

GRONAM

Please, Shlemiel, don't speak. Just be a spy. (*Making a sign, with a finger across his neck, that* SHLEMIEL's *head will be cut off*) Or you'll find yourself a head shorter. This meeting is adjourned.

End of Scene.

Scene 2

SHLEMIEL *at fork in road, two signs there, one pointing to Gorshkov, the other to Chelm. He stops.*

SHLEMIEL

(*To* AUDIENCE)

Oy, oy, oy! Oy, oy, oy! War turns the world upside down. You meet a stranger, and without a hello, already he's trying to kill you. What could be more upside down than that? I'll tell you what is more upside down: That Shlemiel, the most peaceloving of souls, has become a scout, a spy, a soldier. Upside down, I tell you. Almighty God, please, take me now. Why wait until I'm shot dead? Hold it. Wait. Hold it, Almighty God. Here's a fork in the road. One road leads to Gorshkov and war, the other back to Chelm and . . .

SHLEMIEL *makes the sign that his head will be cut off.*

SHLEMIEL (CONT'D)

I'll just switch the signs and lead our army back to Chelm. What have I got to lose?

SHLEMIEL *switches the signs. End of Scene.*

Scene 3

GRONAM, SHLEMIEL, DOPEY, SENDER, TREITEL, *and*
SHLEMIEL *enter. All but* SHLEMIEL *wield pots and pans for*
weapons.

GRONAM
Stay down. I think we're getting close.

SENDER, DOPEY, *and* TREITEL *follow behind, talking among*
themselves.

SENDER
See, what I did was tell my wife that if she gave me her pan, I'd come
back with a slave from Gorshkov to do all the cooking with it.
TREITEL
That's what I did.

DOPEY
Me too and of course my wife said it was fine.

TREITEL
So did mine.

SENDER
So did mine. But then she raised the pan over her head and said I
also better bring the pan back in the very same shape I took it or
she'd kill me.
DOPEY
Like this.

DOPEY *raises pan.* SENDER *ducks.* DOPEY *laughs.*

TREITEL

Mine too. Just like that. So that's why I decided not to let Zalman the Blacksmith melt it into a sword, for if my wife could kill me with the pan, I could surely use the very same pan to kill our enemies.

SENDER

Good thinking. Because that is what I decided as well.

DOPEY

For which one of us is not more deadly with a pan than his own wife?

SENDER

Not me.

TREITEL

Or me either.

GRONAM

Quiet! There it is. Gorshkov. So quiet, so still, so ripe to be taken.

DOPEY

That's Gorshkov?

GRONAM

Where else? We followed the sign right to it, didn't we?

TREITEL

But it looks just like Chelm.

SENDER

The synagogue looks just like our synagogue.

DOPEY

And the town hall looks just like ours, with the town baths right where our town baths are. Shlemiel, what is the meaning of this?

SHLEMIEL

I came at night, spying just like you told me, Gronam. It was dark. I couldn't see what was what in the town. You told me to find out where it was and that's what I certainly did because here we are.

GRONAM

My people, my people, of course it looks the same, for isn't it written in our Great Books that the world is everywhere the same? So naturally that is why Gorshkov looks like Chelm.

SHLEMIEL

Naturally.

DOPEY

Or it could be some sort of trick to keep us off our guard, if our spy somehow gave away that we were going to attack.

DOPEY *raises pan at cowering* SHLEMIEL.

SHLEMIEL

Help!

GRONAM *stops* DOPEY.

GRONAM

Here's the plan. We will go into the town like normal travelers and figure out what's going on. Just leave your weapons in the bushes.

They leave pots and pans in bushes and enter the town.

SENDER

Look! The streets look exactly like our streets. Schlunka Street intersecting with Schlunka Avenue just like at home. O my God, there's Gelfand the Pickleman, who I owe 35 Zoltys since last winter.

SENDER *hides.*

GRONAM

Don't be foolish, Sender.

SENDER

But I've been avoiding him for months.

GRONAM

Just because you owe him 35 Zlotys in Chelm doesn't mean you owe him 35 Zlotys in Gorshkov too.

SENDER

Really? That's right isn't it? Well, he's gone anyway.

GRONAM

Let's act normally and figure out if our enemy is up to anything.

SENDER

But, Gronam, even the town square looks exactly the same. And so does the marketplace.

TREITEL

Look, Gorshkov even has three beggars exactly like our beggars sitting on a park bench. Let's cross the street. I hate the way they look at me when I don't give them anything.

DOPEY

And look there, in the middle of the marketplace a pear tree. Not an apple, not a plum, a pear tree just like in Chelm.

SENDER

And the worshippers going to the synagogue for evening prayers are the same ones who worship in Chelm. You'd think the observant would vary from place to place. Uh oh . . . Here comes the Rabbi.

RABBI *comes walking up.*

RABBI

Good evening, Gentleman. Back from the war so soon?

GRONAM

Let me handle this.
(*To* RABBI)
What war do you mean, Rabbi?

RABBI

Why the war with our enemy, Gorshkov. The one you declared.

GRONAM

We never declared war. We wanted it to be a surprise to everybody.

RABBI

Nevertheless the news spread like wild fire.

DOPEY

(*Threatening* SHLEMIEL)

Loose lips sink ships.

RABBI

So you were victorious, I trust.

GRONAM

Yes. Yes we were.

RABBI

God must've been with you then. And perhaps you should find a way to be with God this evening in synagogue, for a change.

RABBI *exits*

GRONAM

Shame on us. We must not be very observant in Gorshkov either.

TREITEL, SENDER, *and* DOPEY *huddle then break the huddle.*

TREITEL

Gronam, we know it is written that the world is the same everywhere, but we never expected it to be so much the same.

GRONAM

That just goes to show you: When our Great Books say something they really know what they're talking about.

SENDER

Or maybe these people of Gorshkov are more clever than we gave them credit for and are putting on a big act.

DOPEY

What do you think, Gronam? Should we attack? I think we should attack. Look at them: They're totally unprepared.

GRONAM

Wait a minute. We're coming to our street. I mean the street that looks like our street in Chelm only it's here in Gorshkov.

DOPEY

All the houses exactly the same.

TREITEL

There's the broken fence in front of yours you never bother to fix.

DOPEY

I fix it but a stupid dog keeps breaking it again. I wonder if the animals are the same here. I'd love to get my hands on that dog, wherever he is.

They come up to the houses of three of the SAGES. SENDER'S WIFE's *voice comes from inside.*

SENDER'S WIFE

Moishe, stop that noise. You father leaves so I think I'll get a little peace for a change and now *you* start in with me. Go milk the goat. And don't say later or I'll pull your ears.

SENDER

Will God's wonders never cease? A scolding wife just like mine, nagging a disobedient son named Moishe just like mine, in a house on a street just like mine. And imagine, this Moishe says "Later, Mamala" when told to do something just like mine does.

GRONAM

Amazing. Our Great Books are not called great for nothing.

SENDER'S WIFE

Lazy boy, just like your father. He goes off to some war and leaves everything to me. Just wait until he gets home. I'll show him.

SENDER

Gronam, if we have to attack, can't we do it on a different street?

TREITEL'S WIFE *looks out window and calls.*

TREITEL'S WIFE

Treitel, Treitel, is that my little Treitilla, back from the war safe and sound? Come in, come in to me my love, and let me put a thousand kisses on my great hero's lips. Hurry my darling, for your absence has made me even hungrier for your sweet kisses. Treitilla, Treitilla.

TREITEL

What should I do, Gronam?

TREITEL'S WIFE

Treitilla, O Treitilla.

TREITEL

Tell me what to do. For doing such a thing with a woman who isn't my wife would be wrong according to God's sacred commandments.

TREITEL'S WIFE

Treitilla, Treitilla, I'm waiting for you in our warm bed.

TREITEL

Help me. She's as pretty as my wife. Well . . . almost. I'm weakening.
I want to go in to her.

TREITEL *tries to go in but the others hold him back.*

DOPEY

Surrender, Treitilla? When the attack has just begun, Treitilla? What
are you? A traitor, Treitilla?

GRONAM

Your husband will be home in a little while, Mrs. Treitel. He has to
escort our very nice Chelmite prisoners to jail.

TREITEL'S WIFE

I'll be waiting for you, Treitilla. Hurry home to me.

TREITEL

Whew. Thank you, Gronma, for you saved me from myself. There's
your house, Gronam. I mean the house that's like yours in Chelm,
only it's here in Gorshkov.

GRONAM'S WIFE

Children, Children. Rifkele, Sifkele, Tifkele, and Zifkele. Fendele,
Mendele, Pendele, and Wendele. Come here.

GRONAM

Amazing. Great are our books. All the names exactly the same. But
what about Zendele?

GRONAM'S WIFE

Zendele, you too. Come here children. Your father's out in the street, back from the war. Gronam Ox, get in here.

GRONAM *becomes meek.*

GRONAM

But . . .

GRONAM'S WIFE

Why do you keep standing out there like a dummy staring at me with two glass eyes?

GRONAM

But . . .

GRONAM'S WIFE

What are you now, a big war hero? Or the statue of a war hero? Get in here and kiss your children.

GRONAM

But Zlota.

GRONAM'S WIFE

Don't Zlota me.

GRONAM

Your name is Zlota, isn't it?

GRONAM'S WIFE

Of course, what is wrong with you that you would forget my name?

GRONAM
Well, just checking.

GRONAM'S WIFE
Why, on God's Earth?

GRONAM
Well, I was just making sure.

GRONAM'S WIFE
I hope you haven't forgotten other things like my pan.

GRONAM *starts to exit.*

DOPEY
Where are you going, Gronam?

GRONAM
To get this Zlota her pan.

DOPEY
At last, the attack!

GRONAM
No, I'm going in to this Zlota.

DOPEY
What? You? Surrendering? But why?

GRONAM

Because I always listened to my Zlota in Chelm, since a wise man marries wisely, and I don't see why I should stop listening to this Zlota in Gorshkov.

DOPEY

I don't like these people. I say we attack right now.

GRONAM

No. Here are my orders. All of you must go to your houses, or to the houses that are like the ones you live in in Chelm. Go into them for now without attacking, resume your lives and we'll figure this out at our special emergency council meetings. For I think we have stumbled upon one of the great mysteries of creation. A double world. And if things are as I think they are, I want to meet the Gronam Ox who is just like me when he comes back from attacking our village of Chelm.

CHELMITES *fetch weapons, go into houses.* SHLEMIEL *writes.*

SHLEMIEL

(*To* AUDIENCE)

So the brave soldiers of Chelm retrieve their weapons and go into the houses of Gorshkov to wait and wait and a year later, they are waiting still but their enemy twins never arrive. Though the problem does still keep coming up at emergency council meetings.

A council meeting as at beginning of play.

DOPEY

Is it time to attack yet, Gronam?

GRONAM

No, no, not yet. We must carry on as we have been and keep on meeting to ponder this great mystery. Because sometimes I feel we're very close to an answer, sometimes I feel the fog of this mystery is about to lift and we will have a very great revelation. But, and write this down Shlemiel, you must admit that we did solve the problem we set out to solve: For once we were poor in Chelm and, now that we are in Gorshkov, we are poor in Chelm no more.

CHELMITES ALL

Hooray for Gronam Ox! Hooray!

End of play.

The Author Speaks!

How does the Chelmites' belief in the written word, such as council decrees, road signs, and the wisdom in books, influence the plot of the play?

Shlemiel is the most normal character in the play. How is he different from the others?

Do the Chelmites ever believe they are foolish? Why not? What is it in people that prevents them from seeing their own foolishness when it is so obvious to others?

Chico Marx once joked, "Who are you going to believe, me or your own eyes?" Discuss.

Make up a normal question (similar to those asked by the ordinary citizens at the beginning of the play) and then create a silly, semi-wise Chelmite answer.

Did you ever, as a younger person, come up with an idea or scheme that seems very foolish to you now? Describe.

Contributors' Notes

Frances Payne Adler is the author of five books: two poetry collections: *The Making of a Matriot* (Red Hen Press, 2003) and *Raising the Tents* (Calyx Books, 1993); and three collaborative poetry-photography books and exhibitions with photographer Kira Carrillo Corser: *When The Bough Breaks: Pregnancy and The Legacy of Addiction* (NewSage Press, 1993), *Struggle To Be Borne* (San Diego State University Press, 1987), and *Home Street Home* (Red Cross, 1984), that have traveled the country, showing in galleries and state capitol buildings. Their most recent exhibition, "A Matriot's Dream: Health Care For All," showed on Capitol Hill in Washington, D.C. It is on permanent loan to the Universal Health Care Action Network and can be viewed on-line at www.matriot.org. Most recently, Adler co-edited *Fire and Ink: An Anthology of Social Action Writing* (University of Arizona Press, 2009) with poet Diana Garcia and fiction writer Debra Busman. Her awards include a California State Senate Award for Artistic and Social Collaboration, a National Endowment for the Arts Regional Award, and the New Millennium Obama Award. Adler is a professor and founder of the Creative Writing and Social Action Program at California State University Monterey Bay.

Erinn Batykefer was born in Pittsburgh, Pennsylvania during one of the coldest Januaries on record and grew up dividing her time between Northland Public Library, where she worked as a page (read: hid in the stacks and read voraciously, ears pricked for the sound of footsteps and heart pounding at the very thought of getting caught), and the Allegheny River, where she learned to row. Erinn attended the University of Delaware where she studied painting and ceramics before switching majors to concentrate on writing. In 2004, she graduated summa cum laude with a BA in English/Creative Writing and Art History and went on to earn her MFA in poetry from the University of Wisconsin-Madison, where she was a Martha Meier Renk Distinguished Poetry Fellow.

Elizabeth Bradfield grew up in the Pacific Northwest and has since called Cape Cod and Alaska home. She is the author of two poetry collections, *Interpretive*

Work (2008) and *Approaching Ice* (2010). *The Atlantic Monthly, Poetry,* and *Field* have published her poems, as well as the anthologies *Best New Poets 2006* and *Joyful Noise: An Anthology of American Spiritual Poetry.* Bradfield's awards include several Pushcart Prize nominations, a scholarship at the Bread Loaf Writer's Conference, and a Wallace Stegner Fellowship. She holds an MFA from the University of Alaska Anchorage and is founder and editor of *Broadsided.* When not writing, she works as a web designer and naturalist.

Gaylord Brewer's most recent books are the poetry collection *The Martini Diet* (Dream Horse Press, 2008; winner of the 2006 Orphic Prize) and the comic novella *Octavius the 1st* (Red Hen Press, 2008). Red Hen will publish *Give Over, Graymalkin,* his eighth book of poetry, in 2011. His critical works include *David Mamet and Film* (McFarland, 1993) and *Charles Bukowski* (Macmillan, 1997). He has published 700+ poems in journals and anthologies such as *Best American Poetry* and *The Bedford Introduction to Literature,* and his plays have been staged in Chicago, Columbus, Nashville, New York, and Valdez, Alaska. Among his recent residencies were Can Serrat and the Fundación Valparaíso, both in Spain. Brewer teaches at Middle Tennessee State University, where he founded and edits the journal *Poems & Plays,* and in the low-residency MFA program at Murray State University. He's also taught in Russia, Kenya, and the Czech Republic.

Ron Carlson is the author of ten books of fiction, most recently *The Signal,* a novel. He directs the graduate program in fiction at UC Irvine.

Camille T. Dungy is the author of *Suck on the Marrow* (Red Hen Press, 2010) and *What to Eat, What to Drink, What to Leave for Poison* (Red Hen Press, 2006), a finalist for the PEN Center USA 2007 Literary Award and the Library of Virginia 2007 Literary Award. Dungy has received fellowships from organizations including the National Endowment for the Arts, the Virginia Commission for the Arts, Cave Canem, Bread Loaf, the Dana Award, and the American Antiquarian Society. Dungy is Associate Professor in the Creative Writing Department at San Francisco State

University. Editor of *Black Nature: Four Centuries of African American Nature Poetry* (University of Georgia Press, 2009), she is co-editor of *From the Fishouse: An Anthology of Poems that Sing, Rhyme, Resound, Syncopate, Alliterate, and Just Plain Sound Great* (Persea Books, 2009) and assistant editor of *Gathering Ground: A Reader Celebrating Cave Canem's First Decade* (University of Michigan Press, 2006). Her poems have been published widely in anthologies and print and online journals.

Bart Edelman was born in Paterson, New Jersey in 1951 and spent his childhood in Teaneck. He received his undergraduate and graduate degrees from Hofstra University. He is currently a professor of English at Glendale College, where he edits *Eclipse, A Literary Journal*. He was awarded grants and fellowships from the United States Department of Education, the University of Southern California, and the L.B.J. School of Public Affairs at the University of Texas at Austin, conducting literary research in India, Egypt, Nigeria, and Poland. His poetry has appeared in newspapers and journals, as well as textbooks and anthologies, published by City Lights Books, Etruscan Press, Harcourt Brace, McGraw-Hill, Prentice Hall, Simon & Schuster, Thomson/Heinle, and the University of Iowa Press. He teaches poetry workshops across the United States and was Poet-in-Residence at Monroe College of the State University of New York. Collections of his work include *Crossing the Hackensack* (1993), *Under Damaris' Dress* (1996), *The Alphabet of Love* (1999), *The Gentle Man* (2001), and *The Last Mojito* (2005). He lives in Pasadena, California.

Ed Falco is a novelist, short story writer, playwright, and author of literary and experimental short fictions and new media compositions. His books include the short story collections *Acid* and *Burning Man* and the novels *Saint John of the Five Boroughs* and *Wolf Point*. He is the recipient of an NEA Fellowship in Fiction, the Robert Warren Penn Prize in Poetry, and a Virginia Commission for the Arts fellowship in playwriting. Ed lives in Blacksburg, Virginia, where he is the director of the MFA Program in Creative Writing at Virginia Tech.

Kate Gale, 2005–2006 President of PEN USA and president of American Composers Forum/LA, writes poetry, novels, and librettos. Kate Gale has taken the road less travelled. Rather than become a writer with a tenure-track job, she became a writer with two small children. Rather than mourn the lack of literary community in her adopted city of Los Angeles, she decided to create one in the form of Red Hen Press, Los Angeles' literary jewel, *The Los Angeles Review*, a literary magazine, the Ruskin Art Club Poetry Series, the Geffen reading series, and a Writers in the Schools program for underserved communities. At forty, she completed her PhD in literature from Claremont Graduate University, ran her first marathon, and climbed Mt. Whitney, the tallest mountain in the lower forty-eight. Kate Gale's *Rio de Sangre,* an opera with Don Davis, was performed in part at Disney Hall, November of 2005, and her opera *Paradises Lost* was performed in part at the New York City Opera in May of 2006. With publications including five collections of poetry, a novel, and a children's book, for Kate, the journey has just begun. She has poetry, a novella, and new librettos in process, a literary community to energize, and new writers to mentor. May all the ink-stained wenches be so lucky.

Charles Hood is a Fulbright scholar in ethnopoetics and a contributing editor to the *Los Angeles Review*. Hood is also a research associate at the Getty, the Huntington, the Natural History Museum in London, and the Center for Land Use Interpretation, with whom he also has been Artist in Residence. Previous books include *Red Sky, Red Water*, a book about John Wesley Powell and the Colorado River, a rain forest book called *Xopilote Cantos*, and *The Half-Life of Salt: Voices from the* Enola Gay.

Douglas Kearney's first full-length collection of poems, *Fear, Some*, was published in 2006 by Red Hen Press. His second manuscript, *The Black Automaton*, was chosen by Catherine Wagner for the National Poetry Series and published by Fence Books in 2009. In 2008, he was honored with a Whiting Writers Award. Also a librettist, he has collaborated with the composer Anne LeBaron on the opera *Sucktion*, which received a MAP Fund grant and premiered at the New Original Works Festival in Los Angeles in 2008, and on *Mordake* with composer Erling Wold, which premiered in

2008 at the San Francisco International Arts Festival. An Idyllwild and Cave Canem fellow, Kearney has performed his poetry at the Public Theatre, Orpheum, and the World Stage. His poems have appeared in journals such as *Callaloo, jubilat, nocturnes, Ninth Letter, Washington Square*, and *Gulf Coast*. Kearney teaches at California Institute of the Arts.

Ron Koertge grew up in an old mining town in Illinois, on the banks of the Mississippi River. He has lived in California for many years and has been on the faculty of Pasadena City College for more than 35 years. He also teaches in the MFA Writing for Children and Young Adults Program at Hamline University. He is the author of several acclaimed novels, including *The Arizona Kid*, *Stoner & Spaz*, and *Strays*, all of which were ALA Best Books for Young Adults.

Lisa C. Krueger has published two books of poetry and a series of interactive journals related to psychology and creativity. Her poetry has appeared in numerous publications. As a clinical psychologist, she maintains a private therapy practice focused on women's issues, writing therapy, and the role of creativity in wellness. She lives in Pasadena.

Sebastian Matthews is the author of the memoir *In My Father's Footsteps* and co-editor, with Stanley Plumly, of *Search Party: Collected Poems of William Matthews*. Matthews lives with his wife and son in Asheville, North Carolina, where he teaches part-time at Warren Wilson College and the Great Smokies Writing Program and edits *Rivendell*, a place-based literary journal.

Deena Metzger is a novelist, poet, essayist, and storyteller seeking to map the imaginal realms. She is an explorer of the deeper meaning and manifestations of Story. She works as a peace builder, healer, and medicine woman. Deena is the author of many works, including *Ruin and Beauty: New and Selected Poems*, *Grief Into Vision: A Council*, *Entering the Ghost River: Meditations on the Theory and Practice of Healing*, *Tree: Essays and Pieces*, *Writing For Your Life: A Guide and Companion to the Inner Worlds*, and the novels *The Other Hand*, *Doors*, and *What Dinah Thought*. She co-edited *Intimate Nature: The Bond Between Women and Animals*. She is known for her exuberant "Warrior" poster that illustrates the triumph over breast cancer.

Dennis Must is the author of two short story collections: *Oh, Don't Ask Why* (Red Hen Press, 2007) and *Banjo Grease, Selected Stories* (Creative Arts Book Company, 2000), plus a forthcoming novel, *The World's Smallest Bible*, to be published by Red Hen Press. His plays have been performed Off-Off-Broadway and his fiction has appeared in numerous anthologies and literary reviews journals. He resides in Salem, Massachusetts.

Miriam Sagan was born in Manhattan, New York. She holds a BA with honors from Harvard University and an MA in Creative Writing from Boston University. She lived on the coastal extremes of San Francisco and Martha's Vineyard before settling in Santa Fe in 1984. Sagan is the recipient of a grant from The Barbara Deming Foundation/Money for Women.

Greg Sanders's book of short stories, *Motel Girl*, was published by Red Hen Press in 2008. His writing has also appeared in numerous magazines and journals, including *The Los Angeles Review, Essays & Fictions,* and *The Warwick Review*. Greg lives in New York City.

Shelley Savren, author of *The Common Fire* (Red Hen Press, 2004), holds an MFA from Antioch University Los Angeles. She is the recipient of nine California Arts Council Artist in Residence grants, two National Endowment for the Arts regional grants, and five artist fellowships from the City of Ventura. She also received first place in the 1994 John David Johnson Memorial Poetry Award and a nomination for a Pushcart Prize. She has taught poetry writing workshops at a maximum security men's prison, juvenile detention centers, a homeless shelter, a school for emotionally disturbed adolescents, a women's center, and numerous other facilities and at every grade level through the California Poets in the Schools. She lives in Ventura, California and is a full-time English professor at Oxnard College. The Midwest Book Review writes: "*The Common Fire* showcases this remarkable talent and will aptly serve to introduce a whole new audience of readers to a storytelling poetry." Marge Piercy writes: "Shelley Savren's poems in *The Common Fire* are warm and direct, full of the stuff of daily life, family life, joy and pleasure and grief and pain we can all identify with in poems that carry a strong emotional weight." Li-Young Lee writes: "These are poems of earnest storytelling and fond description. Nostalgia for gone worlds and affection for the evanescing present are the subjects and inspirations for this volume. A pleasure to read."

Steven Schutzman is a playwright and fiction writer, the author of nine published books and of numerous plays and stories in literary journals including *The Pushcart Prize, TriQuarterly, Alaska Quarterly Review, Painted Bride Quarterly, Third Coast, Scene 4, Gargoyle, Night Train*, and the new anthology *The Art of the One Act*. More than thirty different plays of his have been produced at such theatres as New Jersey Repertory, Cleveland Public, Baltimore Theatre Project, Rochester Repertory, Circus Theatricals, and Revolution Theatre in Chicago among many others. He is a five-time recipient of Maryland State Arts Council Individual Artist Grant Awards and a three-time top tier finalist for the Eugene O'Neill Center National Playwrights Conference. His one-act "Tree Man" won first prize in the First Stage L.A. One-Act Contest (2004). His full-length play *A Question of Water* was chosen as the unanimous, inaugural selection for the Across the Generations New Jewish Play Festival, 2010.

Julie Shigekuni is the author of three novels: *A Bridge Between Us* (Anchor/Double-day, 1995), *Invisible Gardens* (St. Martin's Press, 2003), and *Unending Nora* (Red Hen Press, 2008). Her fiction has been translated into German, Swedish, Danish, and Norwegian. Shigekuni was a finalist for the Barnes & Noble Discover Great New Writers Award and the recipient of the PEN Oakland Josephine Miles Award for Excellence in Literature. She has received a Henfield Award and an American Japanese Literary Award for her writing. Shigekuni received her BA from CUNY Hunter College and her MFA from Sarah Lawrence College. She is currently at work on a collection of inter-connected short stories and a 60-minute video documentary, *Manju Mammas &*

the *An-Pan Brigade*, for which she has received funding from the California Council for the Humanities and the Skirball Foundation and sponsorship from Visual Communications, an all-Asian media network. She teaches fiction and Asian American Literature at the University of New Mexico and lives in Corrales, New Mexico, with her husband and three young daughters.

Peggy Shumaker grew up in Tucson, Arizona, in the Sonoran desert. She has lived much of her adult life in Interior Alaska, where she taught at University of Alaska Fairbanks. Her poems spring from hidden sources—rivers beneath arroyos, inside glaciers, under the ocean. Her books of poems include *Blaze, Underground Rivers,* and *Gnawed Bones.* Her lyrical memoir *Just Breathe Normally* deals with putting life back together after major injuries from a bicycle wreck. Please visit her website at www.peggyshumaker.com.

Maurya Simon is the author of *The Enchanted Room* and *Days of Awe* (Copper Canyon Press, 1986, 1989), *Speaking in Tongues* (Gibbs Smith, 1990), *The Golden Labyrinth* (University of Missouri Press, 1995), *A Brief History of Punctuation* (Sutton Hoo Press, 2002), and *Weavers,* a collaborative work with Los Angeles artist Baila Goldenthal (Blackbird Press, 2003). Simon is the recipient of a 2002 Visiting Artist Fellowship from the American Academy in Rome, a 1999–2000 NEA Fellowship in poetry, a University Award from the Academy of American Poets, the Celia B. Wagner and Lucille Medwick Memorial Awards from the Poetry Society of America, and a Fulbright-Indo-American Fellowship. Simon has been a fellow at Hawthornden Castle in Edinburgh, Scotland and at the Baltic Centre for Writers and Translators in Visby, Sweden, as well as a lecturer at Lund University in Sweden. Her poems have appeared in *The New Yorker, Poetry, TriQuarterly, The Kenyon Review, The Georgia Review, The Gettysburg Review, Grand Street, Agni, Ploughshares, Shenandoah, The Los Angeles Times Book Review, The New England Review,* and in more than twenty-five anthologies. She teaches in the Creative Writing Department at the University of California, Riverside and lives in the Angeles National Forest of the San Gabriel Mountains in Southern California.

Lisa Russ Spaar, Professor of English and Creative Writing at the University of Virginia, is the author of *Satin Cash: Poems* (Persea Books, 2008), *Blue Venus: Poems* (Persea Books, 2004), and *Glass Town: Poems* (Red Hen Press, 1999), for which she received a Rona Jaffe Award for Emerging Women Writers in 2000, as well as two chapbooks. She is editor of *Acquainted With the Night: Insomnia Poems* (Columbia UP, 1999) and *All That Mighty Heart: London Poems* (University of Virginia Press, 2008). Her work is often anthologized and has appeared in many literary quarterlies and journals. Her work appears in *Best American Poetry 2008*, and her awards include a 2009/2010 Guggenheim Fellowship for Poetry, a University of Virginia All-University Teaching Award, and a 2010 Outstanding Faculty Award from the State Council of Higher Education for Virginia.

Douglas Thorpe is the author of *A New Earth*, *Rapture of the Deep*, *Reflections on the Wild in Art*, *Wilderness and the Sacred* (published by Red Hen Press and winner of the David Family Environmental Book Award), and the forthcoming *Wisdom Sings the World: Poetry and the Way of Dwelling* (Codhill Press). He edited the anthology *Work and the Life of the Spirit* (Mercury House Press). He teaches literature at Seattle Pacific University.

Charles Harper Webb's books of poetry include *Reading the Water*, *Liver*, *Tulip Farms and Leper Colonies*, *Hot Popsicles*, *Amplified Dog*, and *Stand Up Poetry: An Expanded Anthology*, which he edited. *Shadow Ball: New and Selected Poems* was published in 2009 by the University of Pittsburgh Press. Among Webb's awards are the Morse Poetry Prize, the Kate Tufts Discovery Award, the Felix Pollock Prize, the Benjamin Saltman Prize, a Whiting Writer's Award, and a Guggenheim Fellowship. A former rock singer/guitarist and psychotherapist, he directs the MFA Program at California State University, Long Beach.

Sholeh Wolpé is the author of *Rooftops of Tehran*, *The Scar Saloon*, and *Sin: Selected Poems of Forugh Farrokhzad*, for which she was awarded the Lois Roth Translation Prize in 2010 by the American Institute of Iranian Studies. Sholeh is the associate editor of *Tablet & Pen: Literary Landscapes from the Modern Middle East* (Norton), the guest editor of *Atlanta Review* (2010 Iran issue), and the poetry editor of the *Levantine Review*, an online journal about the Middle East. Her poems, translations, essays, and reviews have appeared in scores of literary journals, periodicals, and anthologies worldwide and have been translated into several languages. Sholeh was born in Iran and presently lives in Los Angeles.

To the Tunnel's End

Works by Dead People

edited by

Robert Kane

Cover Art by Gustave Doré

Works selected by William Goldstein, Kate Holguin, Chris Konish, & Robert Kane

Contents

Rudyard Kipling

The Law of the Jungle

Just to give you an idea of the immense variety of the Jungle Law, I have translated into verse (Baloo always recited them in a sort of sing-song) a few of the laws that apply to the wolves. There are, of course, hundreds and hundreds more, but these will do for specimens of the simpler rulings.

> Now this is the Law of the Jungle—as old and as true as
>   the sky;
> And the Wolf that shall keep it may prosper, but the Wolf
>   that shall break it must die.
>
> As the creeper that girdles the tree-trunk the Law runneth
>   forward and back—
> For the strength of the Pack is the Wolf, and the strength
>   of the Wolf is the Pack.
>
> Wash daily from nose-tip to tail-tip; drink deeply, but
>   never too deep;
> And remember the night is for hunting, and forget not
>   the day is for sleep.
>
> The jackal may follow the Tiger, but, Cub, when thy
>   whiskers are grown,
> Remember the Wolf is a hunter—go forth and get food
>   of thine own.

Keep peace with the Lords of the Jungle—the Tiger, the
  Panther, the Bear;
And trouble not Hathi the Silent, and mock not the Boar
  in his lair.

When Pack meets with Pack in the Jungle, and neither
  will go from the trail,
Lie down till the leaders have spoken—it may be fair
  words shall prevail.

When ye fight with a Wolf of the Pack, ye must
  fight him alone and afar,
Lest others take part in the quarrel, and the Pack be
  diminished by war.

The Lair of the Wolf is his refuge, and where he has
  made him his home,
Not even the Head Wolf may enter, not even the Council
  may come.

The Lair of the Wolf is his refuge, but where he has
  digged it too plain,
The Council shall send him a message, and so he shall
  change it again.

If ye kill before midnight, be silent, and wake not the
    woods with your bay,
Lest ye frighten the deer from the crops, and the brothers
    go empty away.

Ye may kill for yourselves, and your mates, and your cubs
    as they need, and ye can;
But kill not for pleasure of killing, and SEVEN TIMES NEVER
    KILL MAN.

If ye plunder his Kill from a weaker, devour not all in
    thy pride;
Pack-Right is the right of the meanest; so leave him the
    head and the hide.

The Kill of the Pack is the meat of the Pack. Ye must
    eat where it lies;
And no one may carry away of that meat to his lair, or
    he dies.

The Kill of the Wolf is the meat of the Wolf. He may
    do what he will,
But, till he has given permission, the Pack may not eat
    of that Kill.

Cub-Right is the right of the Yearling. From all of his
    Pack he may claim
Full-gorge when the killer has eaten; and none may
    refuse him the same.

Lair-Right is the right of the Mother. From all of her
    year she may claim
One haunch of each kill for her litter, and none may
    deny her the same.

Cave-Right is the right of the Father—to hunt by himself
    for his own.
He is freed of all calls to the Pack; he is judged by the
    Council alone.

Because of his age and his cunning, because of his gripe
    and his paw,
In all that the Law leaveth open, the word of the Head
    Wolf is Law.

Now these are the Laws of the Jungle, and many and
    mighty are they;
But the head and the hoof of the Law and the haunch
    and the hump is—Obey!

ELLA WHEELER WILCOX

The Pessimist

The pessimistic locust, last to leaf,
Though all the world is glad, still talks of grief.

Edgar Allan Poe

The Raven

Once upon a midnight dreary, while I pondered, weak and weary,
Over many a quaint and curious volume of forgotten lore—
While I nodded, nearly napping, suddenly there came a tapping,
As of some one gently rapping—rapping at my chamber door.
"'Tis some visitor," I muttered, "tapping at my chamber door—
         Only this and nothing more."

Ah, distinctly I remember, it was in the bleak December,
And each separate dying ember wrought its ghost upon the floor.
Eagerly I wished the morrow;—vainly I had sought to borrow
From my books surcease of sorrow—sorrow for the lost Lenore—
For the rare and radiant maiden whom the angels name Lenore—
         Nameless here for evermore.

And the silken sad uncertain rustling of each purple curtain
Thrilled me—filled me with fantastic terrors never felt before;
So that now, to still the beating of my heart, I stood repeating
"'Tis some visitor entreating entrance at my chamber door—
Some late visitor entreating entrance at my chamber door;
         This it is and nothing more."

Presently my soul grew stronger; hesitating then no longer,
"Sir," said I, "or Madam, truly your forgiveness I implore;
But the fact is I was napping, and so gently you came rapping,
And so faintly you came tapping—tapping at my chamber door,
That I scarce was sure I heard you"—here I opened wide the door—
         Darkness there and nothing more.

Deep into that darkness peering, long I stood there wondering, fearing,
Doubting, dreaming dreams no mortal ever dared to dream before;
But the silence was unbroken, and the stillness gave no token,
And the only word there spoken was the whispered word, "Lenore!"
This I whispered, and an echo murmured back the word, "Lenore!"—
        Merely this and nothing more.

Back into the chamber turning, all my soul within me burning,
Soon again I heard a tapping, somewhat louder than before,
"Surely," said I, "surely that is something at my window lattice;
Let me see, then, what thereat is, and this mystery explore—
Let my heart be still a moment, and this mystery explore;—
        'Tis the wind and nothing more."

Open here I flung the shutter, when, with many a flirt and flutter,
In there stepped a stately Raven of the saintly days of yore.
Not the least obeisance made he; not an instant stopped or stayed he;
But, with mien of lord and lady, perched above my chamber door—
Perched upon a bust of Pallas just above my chamber door—
        Perched, and sat, and nothing more.

Then this ebony bird beguiling my sad fancy into smiling,
By the grave and stern decorum of the countenance it wore,
"Though thy crest be shorn and shaven, thou," I said, "art sure no craven,
Ghastly grim and ancient Raven wandering from the Nightly shore—
Tell me what thy lordly name is on the Night's Plutonian shore!"
        Quoth the Raven, "Nevermore."

Much I marvelled this ungainly fowl to hear discourse so plainly,
Though its answer little meaning—little relevancy bore;
For we cannot help agreeing that no living human being
Ever yet was blessed with seeing bird above his chamber door—
Bird or beast upon the sculptured bust above his chamber door,
        With such a name as "Nevermore."

But the Raven, sitting lonely on that placid bust, spoke only
That one word, as if his soul in that one word he did outpour.
Nothing further then he uttered; not a feather then he fluttered—
Till I scarcely more than muttered, "Other friends have flown before—
On the morrow *he* will leave me, as my Hopes have flown before."
        Then the bird said, "Nevermore."

Startled at the stillness broken by reply so aptly spoken,
"Doubtless," said I, "what it utters is its only stock and store,
Caught from some unhappy master, whom unmerciful Disaster
Followed fast and followed faster till his songs one burden bore—
Till the dirges of his Hope the melancholy burden bore
        Of 'Never—nevermore.'"

But the Raven still beguiling all my sad soul into smiling,
Straight I wheeled a cushioned seat in front of bird and bust and door;
Then, upon the velvet sinking, I betook myself to linking
Fancy unto fancy, thinking what this ominous bird of yore—
What this grim, ungainly, ghastly, gaunt and ominous bird of yore
        Meant in croaking "Nevermore."

This I sat engaged in guessing, but no syllable expressing
To the fowl whose fiery eyes now burned into my bosom's core;
This and more I sat divining, with my head at ease reclining
On the cushion's velvet lining that the lamp-light gloated o'er,
But whose velvet violet lining with the lamp-light gloating o'er,
                                        She shall press, ah, nevermore!

Then, methought, the air grew denser, perfumed from an unseen censer,
Swung by Seraphim whose foot-falls tinkled on the tufted floor.
"Wretch," I cried, "thy God hath lent thee—by these angels he hath sent thee
Respite—respite and nepenthe from thy memories of Lenore!
Quaff, oh quaff this kind nepenthe, and forget this lost Lenore!"
                                        Quoth the Raven, "Nevermore."

"Prophet!" said I, "thing of evil!—prophet still, if bird or devil!—
Whether Tempter sent, or whether tempest tossed thee here ashore,
Desolate yet all undaunted, on this desert land enchanted—
On this home by Horror haunted—tell me truly, I implore—
Is there—*is* there balm in Gilead?—tell me—tell me, I implore!"
                                        Quoth the Raven, "Nevermore."

"Prophet!" said I, "thing of evil!—prophet still, if bird or devil!
By that Heaven that bends above us—by that God we both adore—
Tell this soul with sorrow laden if, within the distant Aidenn,
It shall clasp a saintly maiden whom the angels name Lenore—
Clasp a rare and radiant maiden whom the angels name Lenore."
                                        Quoth the Raven, "Nevermore."

"Be that word our sign of parting, bird or fiend!" I shrieked, upstarting—
"Get thee back into the tempest and the Night's Plutonian shore!
Leave no black plume as a token of that lie thy soul hath spoken!
Leave my loneliness unbroken!—quit the bust above my door!
Take thy beak from out my heart, and take thy form from off my door!"
                                        Quoth the Raven, "Nevermore."

And the Raven, never flitting, still is sitting—still is sitting
On the pallid bust of Pallas just above my chamber door;
And his eyes have all the seeming of a Demon's that is dreaming,
And the lamp-light o'er him streaming throws his shadow on the floor;
And my soul from out that shadow that lies floating on the floor
                                        Shall be lifted—nevermore!

CALLIMACHUS

Heraclitus

They told me, Heraclitus, they told me you were dead,
They brought me bitter news to hear and bitter tears to shed.
I wept, as I remembered, how often you and I
Had tired the sun with talking and sent him down the sky.

And now that thou art lying, my dear old Carian guest,
A handful of grey ashes, long long ago at rest,
Still are thy pleasant voices, thy nightingales, awake;
For Death, he taketh all away, but them he cannot take.

Translated by William Johnson Cory

WILLIAM SHAKESPEARE

Sonnet 18

Shall I compare thee to a summer's day?
Thou art more lovely and more temperate:
Rough winds do shake the darling buds of May,
And summer's lease hath all too short a date:
Sometime too hot the eye of heaven shines,
And often is his gold complexion dimm'd,
And every fair from fair sometime declines,
By chance, or nature's changing course untrimm'd:
But thy eternal summer shall not fade,
Nor lose possession of that fair thou ow'st,
Nor shall death brag thou wander'st in his shade,
When in eternal lines to time thou grow'st,
    So long as men can breathe, or eyes can see,
    So long lives this, and this gives life to thee.

Emma Lazarus

The New Colossus

Not like the brazen giant of Greek fame,
With conquering limbs astride from land to land;
Here at our sea-washed, sunset gates shall stand
A mighty woman with a torch, whose flame
Is the imprisoned lightning, and her name
Mother of Exiles. From her beacon-hand
Glows world-wide welcome; her mild eyes command
The air-bridged harbor that twin cities frame.
"Keep, ancient lands, your storied pomp!" cries she
With silent lips. "Give me your tired, your poor,
Your huddled masses yearning to be free,
The wretched refuse of your teeming shore.
Send these, the homeless, tempest-tost to me,
I lift my lamp beside the golden door!"

Unknown

Hymn to the Mother of the Gods

1. Hail to our mother, who caused the yellow flowers to blossom, who scattered the seeds of the maguey, as she came forth from Paradise.
2. Hail to our mother, who poured forth flowers in abundance, who scattered the seeds of the maguey, as she came forth from Paradise.
3. Hail to our mother, who caused the yellow flowers to blossom, she who scattered the seeds of the maguey, as she came forth from Paradise.
4. Hail to our mother, who poured forth white flowers in abundance, who scattered the seeds of the maguey, as she came forth from Paradise.
5. Hail to the goddess who shines in the thorn bush like a bright butterfly.
6. Ho! she is our mother, goddess of the earth, she supplies food in the desert to the wild beasts, and causes them to live.
7. Thus, thus, you see her to be an ever-fresh model of liberality toward all flesh.
8. And as you see the goddess of the earth do to the wild beasts, so also does she toward the green herbs and the fishes.

Translated by Daniel G. Brinton

Unknown

How the Devil Lost His Wager

A peasant, ploughing his field, was panting with fatigue, when the devil appeared before him and said:

"Oh, poor man! you complain of your lot, and with justice; for your labor is not that of a man, but is as heavy as that of a beast of burden. Now I have made a wager that I shall find a contented man; so give me the handle of your plough and the goad of your oxen, that I may do the work for you."

The peasant consenting, the devil touched the oxen and in one turn of the plough all the furrows of the field were opened up and the work finished.

"Is it well done?" asked the devil.

"Yes," replied the man, "but seed is very dear this year."

In answer to this, the devil shook his long tail in the air, and lo, little seeds began to fall like hail from the sky.

"I hope," said the devil, "that I have gained my wager."

"Bah," answered the peasant, "what's the good of that? These seeds might be lost. You do not take into consideration frost, blighting winds, drought, damp, storms, diseases of plants, and other things. How can I judge as yet?"

"Behold," said the devil, "in this box are both sun and rain, take it and use it as you please."

The peasant did so and to very good purpose, for his corn soon ripened and up to that time he had never seen so good a harvest. But the corn of his neighbors had also prospered from the rain and sun.

At harvest time the devil came, and saw that the man was looking with envious eyes at his neighbor's fields where the corn was as good as his own.

"Have you been able to obtain what you desired?" asked the devil.

"Alas!" answered the man, "all the barns will break down under the weight of the sheaves. The grain will be sold at a low price. This fine harvest will make me sit on ashes."

While he was speaking, the devil had taken an ear of corn from the ground and was crushing it in his hand, and as soon as he blew on the grains they all turned into pure gold. The peasant took up one and examined it attentively on all sides, and then in a despairing tone cried out: "Oh, my God! I must spend money to melt all these and send them to the mint."

The devil wrung his hands in despair. He had lost his wager. He could do everything, but he could not make a contented man.

Translated by Cyrus Adler and Allan Ramsey

Mark Twain

An Excerpt from Eve's Diary

SATURDAY—I am almost a whole day old, now. I arrived yesterday. That is as it seems to me. And it must be so, for if there was a day-before-yesterday I was not there when it happened, or I should remember it. It could be, of course, that it did happen, and that I was not noticing. Very well; I will be very watchful now, and if any day-before-yesterdays happen I will make a note of it. It will be best to start right and not let the record get confused, for some instinct tells me that these details are going to be important to the historian some day. For I feel like an experiment, I feel exactly like an experiment; it would be impossible for a person to feel more like an experiment than I do, and so I am coming to feel convinced that that is what I AM—an experiment; just an experiment, and nothing more.

Then if I am an experiment, am I the whole of it? No, I think not; I think the rest of it is part of it. I am the main part of it, but I think the rest of it has its share in the matter. Is my position assured, or do I have to watch it and take care of it? The latter, perhaps. Some instinct tells me that eternal vigilance is the price of supremacy. [That is a good phrase, I think, for one so young.]

Everything looks better today than it did yesterday. In the rush of finishing up yesterday, the mountains were left in a ragged condition, and some of the plains were so cluttered with rubbish and remnants that the aspects were quite distressing. Noble and beautiful works of art should not be subjected to haste; and this majestic new world is indeed a most noble and beautiful work. And certainly marvelously near to being perfect, notwithstanding the shortness of the time. There are too many stars in some places and not enough in others, but that can be remedied presently, no doubt. The moon got loose last night, and slid down and fell out of the scheme—a very great loss; it breaks my heart to think of it. There isn't another thing among the ornaments and decorations that is comparable to it for beauty and finish. It should have been fastened better. If we can only get it back again—

But of course there is no telling where it went to. And besides, whoever gets it will hide it; I know it because I would do it myself. I believe I can be honest in all other matters, but I already begin to realize that the core and center of my nature is love of the beautiful, a passion for the beautiful, and that it would not be safe to trust me with a moon that belonged to another person and that person didn't know I had it. I could give up a moon that I found in the daytime, because I should be afraid some one was looking; but if I found it in the dark, I am sure I should find some kind of an excuse for not saying anything about it. For I do love moons, they are so pretty and so romantic. I wish we had five or six; I would never go to bed; I should never get tired lying on the moss-bank and looking up at them.

Stars are good, too. I wish I could get some to put in my hair. But I suppose I never can. You would be surprised to find how far off they are, for they do not look it. When they first showed, last night, I tried to knock some down with a pole, but it didn't reach, which astonished me; then I tried clods till I was all tired out, but I never got one. It was because I am left-handed and cannot throw good. Even when I aimed at the one I wasn't after I couldn't hit the other one, though I did make some close shots, for I saw the black blot of the clod sail right into the midst of the golden clusters forty or fifty times, just barely missing them, and if I could have held out a little longer maybe I could have got one.

So I cried a little, which was natural, I suppose, for one of my age, and after I was rested I got a basket and started for a place on the extreme rim of the circle, where the stars were close to the ground and I could get them with my hands, which would be better, anyway, because I could gather them tenderly then, and not break them. But it was farther than I thought, and at last I had go give it up; I was so tired I couldn't drag my feet another step; and besides, they were sore and hurt me very much.

I couldn't get back home; it was too far and turning cold; but I found some tigers and nestled in among them and was most adorably comfortable, and their breath was sweet and pleasant, because they live on strawberries. I had never seen a tiger before, but I knew them in a minute by the stripes. If I could have one of those skins, it would make a lovely gown.

Today I am getting better ideas about distances. I was so eager to get hold of every pretty thing that I giddily grabbed for it, sometimes when it was too far off, and sometimes when it was but six inches away but seemed a foot—alas, with thorns between! I learned a lesson; also I made an axiom, all out of my own head—my very first one; THE SCRATCHED EXPERIMENT SHUNS THE THORN. I think it is a very good one for one so young.

I followed the other Experiment around, yesterday afternoon, at a distance, to see what it might be for, if I could. But I was not able to make out. I think it is a man. I had never seen a man, but it looked like one, and I feel sure that that is what it is. I realize that I feel more curiosity about it than about any of the other reptiles. If it is a reptile, and I suppose it is; for it has frowzy hair and blue eyes, and looks like a reptile. It has no hips; it tapers like a carrot; when it stands, it spreads itself apart like a derrick; so I think it is a reptile, though it may be architecture.

I was afraid of it at first, and started to run every time it turned around, for I thought it was going to chase me; but by and by I found it was only trying to get away, so after that I was not timid any more, but tracked it along, several hours, about twenty yards behind, which made it nervous and unhappy. At last it was a good deal worried, and climbed a tree. I waited a good while, then gave it up and went home.

Today the same thing over. I've got it up the tree again.

W.S. Gilbert

Pygmalion and Galatea

An Excerpt from Act I, Scene I

Characters:
PYGMALION, an Athenian sculptor
CYNISCA, his Wife
GALATEA, an animated statue

Scene: PYGMALION's *studio; several classical statues are placed about the room; at the back a cabinet containing a statue of* GALATEA, *before which curtains are drawn concealing the statue.*

PYGMALION

    It all but breathes—therefore it talks aloud!
    It all but moves—therefore it walks and runs!
    It all but lives, and therefore it is life!
    No, no, my love, the thing is cold, dull stone,
    Shaped to a certain form, but still dull stone,
    The lifeless, senseless mockery of life.
    The gods make life, I can make only death!
    Why, my Cynisca, though I stand so well,
    The merest cut-throat, when he plies his trade,
    Makes better death than I with all my skill!

CYNISCA

    Hush, my Pygmalion! the gods are good,
    And they have made thee nearer unto them
    Than other men; this is ingratitude!

PYGMALION

Not so; has not a monarch's second son
More cause for anger that he lacks a throne
Than he whose lot is cast in slavery?

CYNISCA

Not much more cause, perhaps, but more excuse.
Now I must go.

PYGMALION

So soon, and for so long?

CYNISCA

One day, 'twill quickly pass away!

PYGMALION

With those who measure time, by almanacs, no doubt,
But not with him who knows no days save those
Born of the sunlight of Cynisca's eyes;
It will be night with me till she returns.

CYNISCA

Then sleep it through, Pygmalion! But stay,
Thou shalt not pass the weary hours alone;
Now mark thou this—while I'm away from thee,
There stands my only representative;
(*Withdrawing curtains*)
She is my proxy, and I charge you, sir,
Be faithful unto her as unto me!
Into her quietly attentive ear
Pour all thy treasures of hyperbole,

And give thy nimble tongue full license, lest
Disuse should rust its glib machinery;
(*Advancing*)
If thoughts of love should haply crowd on thee,
There stands my other self, tell them to her,
She'll listen well; nay, that's ungenerous,
For she is I, yet lovelier than I,
And hath no temper, sir, and hath no tongue;
Thou hast thy license—make good use of it.
Already I'm half jealous—there!
(*Draws curtain concealing statue*)
It's gone.
The thing is but a statue after all,
And I am safe in leaving thee with her;
Farewell, Pygmalion, till I return.

Exit.

PYGMALION
   "The thing is but a statue after all!"
   Cynisca little thought that in those words
   She touched the key-note of my discontent.
   True, I have powers denied to other men;
   Give me a block of senseless marble—Well,
   I'm a magician, and it rests with me
   To say what kernel lies within its shell;
   It shall contain a man, a woman, a child,
   A dozen men and women if I will.
   So far the gods and I run neck and neck,
   Nay, so far I can beat them at their trade;
   I am no bungler—all the men I make

Are straight limbed fellows, each magnificent
In the perfection of his manly grace;
I make no crook-backs; all my men are gods,
My women, goddesses, in outward form.
But there's my tether—I can go so far,
And go no farther—at that point I stop,
To curse the bonds that hold me sternly back.
To curse the arrogance of those proud gods,
Who say, "Thou shalt be greatest among men,
And yet infinitesimally small!"

GALATEA
(*From behind curtain*)
Pygmalion!

PYGMALION
Who called?

GALATEA
Pygmalion!

PYGMALION *tears away curtain and discovers* GALATEA *alive.*

PYGMALION
Ye gods! It lives!

GALATEA
Pygmalion!

PYGMALION
> It speaks!
> I have my prayer! my Galatea breathes!

GALATEA
> Where am I? Let me speak, Pygmalion;
> Give me thy hand—both hands—how soft and warm!
> Whence came I?

Descends.

PYGMALION
> Why, from yonder pedestal.

GALATEA
> That pedestal! Ah, yes, I recollect.
> There was a time when it was part of me.

PYGMALION
> That time has passed forever, thou art now
> A living, breathing woman, excellent
> In every attribute of womankind.

GALATEA
> Where am I, then?

PYGMALION
> Why, born into the world
> By miracle.

GALATEA
Is this the world?

PYGMALION
It is.

GALATEA
This room?

PYGMALION
This room is portion of a house;
The house stands in a grove, the grove itself
Is one of many, many thousand groves
In Athens.

GALATEA
And is Athens then the world?

PYGMALION
To an Athenian—Yes—

GALATEA
And I am one?

PYGMALION
By birth and parentage, not by descent.

GALATEA
But how came I to be?

PYGMALION
Well—let me see.
Oh—you were quarried in Pentelicus;
I modeled you in clay—my artisans
Then roughed you out in marble—I, in turn,
Brought my artistic skill to bear on you,
And made you what you are—in all but life—
The gods completed what I had begun,
And gave the only gift I could not give.

GALATEA
Then is this life?

PYGMALION
It is.

GALATEA
And not long since
I was a cold, dull stone. I recollect
That by some means I knew that I was stone,
That was the first dull gleam of conscience;
I became conscious of a chilly self,
A cold immovable identity,
I knew that I was stone, and knew no more;
Then, by an imperceptible advance,
Came the dim evidence of outer things,
Seen—darkly and imperfectly—yet seen—
The walls surrounded me, and I, alone,
That pedestal—that curtain—then a voice
That called on Galatea! At that word,
Which seemed to shake my marble to the core,

That which was dim before, came evident.
Sounds, that had hummed around me, indistinct,
Vague, meaningless—seemed to resolve themselves
Into a language I could understand;
I felt my frame pervaded with a glow
That seemed to thaw my marble into flesh;
Its cold hard substance throbbed with active life,
My limbs grew supple, and I moved—I lived!
Lived in the ecstasy of new born life;
Lived in the love of him that fashioned me;
Lived in a thousand tangled thoughts of hope,
Love, gratitude, thoughts that resolved themselves
Into one word, that word, Pygmalion!

Kneels.

PYGMALION

I have no words to tell thee of my joy,
O woman—perfect in thy loveliness.

GALATEA

What is that word? Am I a woman?

PYGMALION

Yes.

GALATEA

Art thou a woman?

PYGMALION

No, I am a man.

GALATEA

What is a man?

PYGMALION

A being strongly framed,
To wait on woman, and protect her from
All ills that strength and courage can avert;
To work and toil for her, that she may rest;
To weep and mourn for her, that she may laugh;
To fight and die for her, that she might live!

GALATEA

I'm glad I am a woman.

He leads her down.

PYGMALION

So am I.

GALATEA

That I escape the pains thou hast to bear?

PYGMALION

That I may undergo those pains for thee.

GALATEA

With whom then wouldst thou fight?

PYGMALION

With any man
Whose word or deed gave Galatea pain.

GALATEA

Then there are other men in this strange world?

PYGMALION

There are indeed.

GALATEA

And other women?

PYGMALION

Yes;
Though for the moment I'd forgotten it;
Yes, other women.

GALATEA

And for all of these
Men work, and toil, and mourn, and weep and fight?

PYGMALION

It is man's duty, if he's called upon,
To fight for all; he works for those he loves.

GALATEA

Then by thy works I know thou lovest me.

PYGMALION

Indeed, I love thee!

GALATEA

With what kind of love?

PYGMALION

I love thee as a sculptor does his work!
(*Aside*)
There is diplomacy in that reply.

GALATEA

My love is different in kind to thine;
I am no sculptor, and I've done no work,
Yet I do love thee; say—what love is mine?

PYGMALION

Tell me its symptoms—then I'll answer thee.

GALATEA

Its symptoms? Let me call them as they come.
A sense that I am made by thee for thee,
That I've no will that is not wholly thine,
That I've no thought, no hope, no enterprise,
That does not own thee as its sovereign;
That I have life, that I may live for thee,
That I am thine—that thou and I are one!
What kind of love is that?

PYGMALION

A kind of love
That I shall run some risk in dealing with.

GALATEA

And why, Pygmalion?

PYGMALION

Such love as thine
A man may not receive, except indeed
From one who is, or is to be, his wife.

GALATEA

Then I will be thy wife.

PYGMALION

That may not be;
I have a wife—the gods allow but one.

GALATEA

Why did the gods then send me here to thee?

PYGMALION

I cannot say—unless to punish me
For unreflecting and presumptuous prayer!
I prayed that thou shouldst live. I have my prayer,
And now I see the fearful consequence
That must attend it!

GALATEA

Yet thou lovest me?

PYGMALION

Who could look on that face and stifle love?

GALATEA

Then I am beautiful?

PYGMALION

Indeed thou art.

GALATEA

I wish that I could look upon myself,
But that's impossible.

PYGMALION

Not so indeed,
This mirror will reflect thy face. Behold!

GALATEA

How beautiful! I am very glad to know
That both our tastes agree so perfectly;
Why, my Pygmalion, I did not think
That aught could be more beautiful than thou,
Till I beheld myself. Believe me, love,
I could look in this mirror all day long.
So I'm a woman.

PYGMALION

There's no doubt of that!

GALATEA

Oh happy maid to be so passing fair!
And happier still Pygmalion, who can gaze,
At will, upon so beautiful a face.

PYGMALION

Hush! Galatea—in thine innocence
Thou sayest things that others would reprove.

GALATEA

    Indeed, Pygmalion; then it is wrong
    To think that one is exquisitely fair?

PYGMALION

    Well, Galatea, it's a sentiment
    That every woman shares with thee;
    They think it—but they keep it to themselves.

GALATEA

    And is thy wife as beautiful as I?

PYGMALION

    No, Galatea, for in forming thee
    I took her features—lovely in themselves—
    And in the marble made them lovelier still.

GALATEA

    Oh! then I'm not original?

PYGMALION

    Well—no—
    That is—thou hast indeed a prototype,
    But though in stone thou didst resemble her,
    In life, the difference is manifest.

GALATEA

    I'm very glad that I am lovelier than she.
    And am I better?

PYGMALION

That I do not know.

GALATEA

Then she has faults.

PYGMALION

Very few indeed;
Mere trivial blemishes, that serve to show
That she and I are of one common kin.
I love her all the better for such faults.

GALATEA

Tell me some faults and I'll commit them now.

PYGMALION

There is no hurry; they will come in time;
Though for that matter, it's a grievous sin
To sit as lovingly as we sit now.

GALATEA

Is sin so pleasant? If to sit and talk
As we are sitting, be indeed a sin,
Why I could sin all day. But tell me, love,
Is this great fault that I'm committing now
The kind of fault that only serves to show
That thou and I are of one common kin?

PYGMALION

Indeed, I'm very much afraid it is.

GALATEA

And dost thou love me better for such fault?

PYGMALION

Where is the mortal that could answer "no"?

GALATEA

Why, then I'm satisfied, Pygmalion;
Thy wife and I can start on equal terms.
She loves thee?

PYGMALION

Very much.

GALATEA

I'm glad of that.
I like thy wife.

PYGMALION

And why?

GALATEA

Our tastes agree.
We love Pygmalion well, and what is more,
Pygmalion loves us both. I like thy wife;
I'm sure we shall agree.

PYGMALION

(*Aside*)
I doubt it much.

GALATEA

Is she within?

PYGMALION

No, she is not within.

GALATEA

But she'll come back?

PYGMALION

Oh, yes, she will come back.

GALATEA

How pleased she'll be to know when she returns,
That there was some one here to fill her place.

PYGMALION

Yes, I should say she'd be extremely pleased.

GALATEA

Why, there is something in thy voice which says
That thou art jesting. Is it possible
To say one thing and mean another?

PYGMALION

Yes,
It's sometimes done.

GALATEA

How very wonderful!
So clever!

PYGMALION

    And so very useful.

GALATEA

    Yes.
    Teach me the art.

PYGMALION

    The art will come in time.
    My wife will not be pleased; there—that's the truth.

GALATEA

    I do not think that I shall like thy wife.
    Tell me more of her.

PYGMALION

    Well—

GALATEA

    What did she say
    When last she left thee?

PYGMALION

    Humph! Well, let me see;
    Oh! true, she gave thee to me as my wife,—
    Her solitary representative;
    She feared I should be lonely till she came.
    And counseled me, if thoughts of love should come,
    To speak those thoughts to thee, as I am wont
    To speak to her.

GALATEA

That's right.

PYGMALION

But when she spoke
Thou wast a stone, now thou art flesh and blood,
Which makes a difference.

GALATEA

It's a strange world;
A woman loves her husband very much,
And cannot brook that I should love him too;
She fears he will be lonely till she comes,
And will not let me cheer his loneliness;
She bids him breathe his love to senseless stone,
And when that stone is brought to life—be dumb!
It's a strange world, I cannot fathom it.

PYGMALION

(*Aside*)
Let me be brave and put an end to this.
Come Galatea—till my wife returns,
My sister shall provide thee with a home;
Her house is close at hand.

GALATEA

Send me not hence, Pygmalion; let me stay.

PYGMALION

It may not be.
Come, Galatea, we shall meet again.

GALATEA

Do with me as thou wilt, Pygmalion!
But we shall meet again?—and very soon?

PYGMALION

Yes, very soon.

GALATEA

And when thy wife returns,
She'll let me stay with thee?

PYGMALION

I do not know.
(*Aside*)
Why should I hide the truth from her?
(*Aloud*)
Alas! I may not see thee then.

GALATEA

Pygmalion!
What fearful words are these?

PYGMALION

The bitter truth.
I may not love thee; I must send thee hence.

GALATEA

Recall those words, Pygmalion, my love!
Was it for this that heaven gave me life?
Pygmalion, have mercy on me; see,
I am thy work, thou hast created me;

The gods have sent me to thee. I am thine!
Thine! only, and unalterably thine!
This is the thought with which my soul is charged.
Thou tellest me of one who claims thy love,
That thou hast love for her alone. Alas!
I do not know these things; I only know
That heaven has sent me here to be with thee.
Thou tellest me of duty to thy wife,
Of vows that thou wilt love but her. Alas!
I do not know these things; I only know
That heaven, who sent me here, has given me
One all absorbing duty to discharge—
To love thee, and to make thee love again.

PYGMALION *takes her in his arms, and embraces her passionately.*

Contributors' Epitaphs:

Cyrus Adler: "... death was preferable to the annoyance he had received ..." Died April 7, 1940.

Daniel G. Brinton: "All must agree to this, though they may differ widely as to what such a mental state may be; whether one of pleasurable activity, or that of the Buddhist hermit who sinks into a trance by staring at his navel, or that of the Trappist monk whose occupations are the meditation of death and digging his own grave." Died July 31, 1899.

Callimachus: "Death, he taketh all away, but them he cannot take." Died a long, long time ago.

William Johnson Cory: "Death does us wrong, the fates are cross; [n]or will this age repair the loss." Died in 1892.

Gustave Doré: "The present volume shows Gustave Doré as a master of the grotesque; and the Publishers appeal to the Public, to whom the volume is offered, confident in the expectation that the high estimate formed by those to whom these Sketches are already familiar, will be corroborated by the general verdict." Died January 23, 1883.

W.S. Gilbert: "Is life a boon? If so, it must befall [t]hat Death, whene'er he call, [m]ust call too soon." Died May 29th, 1911.

Rudyard Kipling: "Thou hast untied the feet of Death, and he will follow thy trail till thou diest. Thou hast taught Man to kill!" Died January 18, 1936.

Emma Lazarus: "Is death more terrible, more hateworthy, [m]ore bitter than dishonor?" Died November 19th, 1887.

Edgar Allan Poe: "I could not love except where Death [w]as mingling his with Beauty's breath—" Died October 7, 1849.

Allan Ramsey: "What might be his punishment he did not know—most probably death." Died January 7, 1758.

Mark Twain: "I came in with Halley's Comet in 1835. It is coming again next year, and I expect to go out with it. It will be the greatest disappointment of my life if I don't go out with Halley's Comet. The Almighty has said, no doubt: 'Now here are these two unaccountable freaks; they came in together, they most go out together.'" Died April 21, 1910.

Unknown: "Can you say whether the head was cut off before or after death?"

Ella Wheeler Wilcox: "When that day comes to you, and Death, unmasking, [s]hall bar your path, and say, 'Behold the end,' [w]hat are the questions that he will be asking [a]bout your past? Have you considered, friend? I think he will not chide you for your sinning, [n]or for your creeds or dogmas will he care; [h]e will but ask, *From your life's first beginning [h]ow many burdens have you helped to bear?*' Died October 30, 1919."